The Last Words of Jesus to His Disciples
Enduring Lessons of Faith, Hope, and Love

by

Floyd Bland

Copyright © 2020 by Floyd Bland. All rights reserved. No part of this book may be reproduced, transmitted, or stored in any form except as permitted under U.S. copyright laws. Address requests for permission to info@notwm.org.

This book has been written for Christian inspirational purposes only. It is not intended to provide legal or clinical advice to replace the services of qualified professionals. No liability is assumed for loss or damage from its content since readers are to assume full responsibility for their own personal safety and well-being.

Some content is recreated from the author's memory and altered to maintain anonymity. Any resemblance to actual persons, entities, or locales is coincidental.

Scripture quotations marked (AKJV) are taken from The Authorized (King James) Version. Rights in the Authorized Version in the United Kingdom are vested in the Crown. Reproduced by permission of the Crown's patentee, Cambridge University Press.

Scripture quotations marked (NKJV) are from the New King James Version®. Copyright © 1982 by Thomas Nelson. Used by permission. All rights reserved.

Scripture quotations marked (NIV) are from the Holy Bible, New International Version®, NIV®. Copyright © 1973, 1978, 1984, 2011 by Biblica, Inc.

™ Used by permission of Zondervan. All rights reserved worldwide. www.zondervan.com The "NIV" and "New International Version" are trademarks registered in the United States Patent and Trademark Office by Biblica, Inc. ™

Scripture quotations marked (NLT) are taken from the Holy Bible, New Living Translation, copyright ©1996, 2004, 2007, 2013, 2015 by Tyndale House Foundation. Used by permission of Tyndale House Publishers, Inc., Carol Stream, Illinois 60188. All rights reserved.

Some chapter heading images are licensed under ©Graphics Factory.com and are used by permission.

Content by Randy Hoyt/TypeGreek.com is released by permission under the Creative Commons 2.5 License. To review a copy of the license, please visit www.creativecommons.org.

Images licensed by Ministry-To-Children.com are bound under the Creative Commons Attribution 4.0 International License. To view a copy of this license, send a letter to Creative Commons, PO Box 1866, Mountain View, CA 94042, USA, or visit http://creativecommons.org/licenses/by/4.0/.

ISBN-13: 978-1-7325342-3-0
Library of Congress Control Number: 2020918066

Let Not Your Heart Be Troubled!

Contents

With Gratitude vii
Preface: On Finishing Well 1
    Musing God's Grace and Mercy 1
Chapter One: A Busy Week of Preparation 5
    One Final Opportunity 5
    Unbelievable Altruism 10
Chapter Two: Presenting A New Covenant 20
    A Lesson on Humility 20
    A New Commandment 23
    In Remembrance of Me 26
Chapter Three: One Distinct Person and Plan 32
    Let Not Your Heart be Troubled 32
    The Way, Truth, and Life 36
    The Helper Is on the Way 39
    My Peace I Leave with You 42
Chapter Four: True Vine's Chosen Ones 48
    I Am the Vine—You are the Branches 48
    I Have Chosen You 54
    The World's Opposition 69
Chapter Five: The Helper's Mission and Work 75
    The Helper's Reproving Work 75
    Overcoming the World 84
Chapter Six: Jesus' Intercessory Prayer 94
    Jesus Prays to be Glorified 94
    Jesus Prays for His Disciples 99
    Jesus Prays for His Followers 105
About the Author.. 110

With Gratitude

I thank God for His love, grace, and mercy always, for they allow me to experience the abundant, eternal life He promises to all who trust in Him, through our Lord and Savior Jesus Christ.

I also thank God for my supportive family whose love and encouragement made me who I am today. They have given me the latitude to pursue my calling to "strengthen the brethren, and to bear eternal fruit for Christ" to the best of my ability.

In addition, I thank God for those unsung heroes and inspiring role models who have prayed for and assisted me over the years.

Moreover, I thank God for Pam Lagomarsino of Above the Pages Editorial Services and Paramita Bhattacharjee of Creative Paramita Book Cover Designs for their professionalism and expertise in this book's preparation for publication.

Preface

Preface:
On Finishing Well

Musing God's Grace and Mercy

When I reflect on my Christian journey, I marvel at how the Lord extends His grace and mercy toward us. He does this despite the human flaws and incompletions that we, who "see through a glass darkly" (1 Corinthians 13:12), share equally. I am astounded at how He protects, provides, and preserves all His children…*including me.*

I can trace my Christian roots to three marvelous people who led me to the Lord Jesus Christ and helped me understand His impeccable Kingdom of God (Kingdom) living. Mom, Dad, and Grandma were more than capable as instruments the Lord used to raise me in His "nurture and admonition" (Ephesians 6:4).

They introduced me to the Lord very early in life so that long before I attended public schools, we were attending church, praying, and having family devotions together. We also shared many insightful discussions where they explained fundamental biblical truths in a way I could understand, embrace, and grow from spiritually.

My parents were extremely reverent when it came to the Bible's inspiration and content. I marvel at how "unlearned" they were by our educational standards (only one completed high school), yet they were extremely competent students and teachers of the Bible. Their wonderful influence on my life helped me comprehend, engage, and apply the Scriptures to my daily life, which facilitated my spiritual progress and growth. They modeled an exceptional Christian character consistently as well. No one is perfect. However, they were notably authentic about living a Christian life and maintaining a Christian home.

Proverbs 22:6 (NLT) tells us to direct our children "onto the right path, and when they are older, they will not leave it." Thus, when I met my wife and started my family, I incorporated much of what I learned during those formative years. Together, we share a reverence for God and His Word—a vigilance to be ready for Jesus' return and personal, inspirational stories of God's faithfulness.

Ultimately, the Lord has not failed to demonstrate His love, mercy, and faithfulness in "real-time," using my beloved wife and family. Thus, Psalm 37:25 (NLT) has been a living reality for me,

> Once I was young, and now I am old. Yet I have never seen the godly abandoned or their children begging for bread.

These experiences inspire me to write about our Savior and Redeemer, who finished well, especially on His last evening presented in John chapters 13–17,

Chapter 13
- A Lesson on Humility
- A New Commandment
- In Remembrance of Me

Chapter 14
- Let Not Your Heart be Troubled
- The Way, Truth, and Life
- The Helper Is on the Way
- My Peace I Leave with You

Chapter 15
- I Am the Vine—You are the Branches
- I Have Chosen You
- The World's Opposition

Chapter 16
- The Helper's Reproving Work
- Overcoming the World

Chapter 17
- Jesus Prays to be Glorified
- Jesus Prays for His Disciples
- Jesus Prays for His Followers

Over the next few pages, we will explore the many wonderful lessons Jesus taught on that incredible evening. The people, entities, and places our Lord will encounter or discuss are very important. Thus, I have capitalized applicable nouns and pronouns for lesson clarity and consistency.

Chapter One

Chapter One:
A Busy Week of Preparation

One Final Opportunity

It was on a Thursday evening of a busy Passion Week during the festive Feasts of Passover and Unleavened Bread (the fourteenth through the twenty-first day of Nisan, the first month of the Jewish calendar).[1]

During this week of consecration and celebration, Jews from around the world converged on Jerusalem to increase the city's population exponentially,

> The number of permanent residents in Jerusalem that Jesus knew was about six hundred thousand. A conservative estimate of the vast multitude of Passover pilgrims is about two million, who swelled the city's population to almost four times its normal size.[2]

All Jewish males were required to attend the Passover and the Feast of Unleavened Bread, the Feast of Weeks (Pentecost), and the Feast of Booths (Tabernacles).[3]

Passover and Unleavened Bread were associated with the Children of Israel's release from four-hundred years of Egyptian slavery (Exodus

12:1–13:16, 23:17, 34:23). Festive revelers, musicians, and celebrators packed the streets with song, dance, and reverie.

However, Jesus' last week on earth, which culminated with what we observe today as Palm Sunday, Good Friday, and Easter went like this:

Sunday

The week began on our Palm Sunday, with Jesus' Triumphal Entry into His beloved Jerusalem. He presents Himself as the long-awaited Messiah riding a donkey. Crowds gathered to lay palm branches and their outer clothing in His path shouting,

> Hosanna to the Son of David! Blessed is He who comes in the name of the Lord! Hosanna in the highest heaven! (Matthew 21:9 NIV).

Jesus did not ride a horse, as would a conquering hero. Instead, He rides the donkey's colt, a symbol of peace, to present Himself as God's humble emissary sent to redeem a fallen humanity. His calculated actions fulfill the Messianic prophesies of Isaiah 62:11 and Zechariah 9:9.

This same day, Jesus visits the Temple where He heals the blind and lame gathered there. It was getting late in the day, so He and the Disciples retire to nearby Bethany.

Monday

This was a day of controversy and teaching at the Jerusalem Temple. Jesus begins by chasing the moneychangers from the Temple complex (for the second time), which enraged the religious leaders.

Then, certain Greeks request a private audience with the Lord, and He foretells of His death and resurrection.

Their inquiry represents a major shift in Jesus' ministry. Events from this day forward would offer non-Jews (Gentiles) access to the Covenant God of Israel through faith Jesus Christ as Savior and Lord. Ironically, Gentiles would embrace Him while many of His own people rejected Him still,

> He came to his own people, and even they rejected him. But to all who believed him and accepted him, he gave the right to become Children of God (John 1:11–12 NLT).

Jesus also predicts how His impending death on the cross and His glorious resurrection will draw both Jews and Gentiles to Him,

> The time for judging this world has come, when Satan, the ruler of this world, will be cast out. And when I am lifted up from the earth, I will draw everyone to myself (John 12:31–32 NLT).

Tuesday

This was Jesus' most active day as He confronts religious leaders at the Temple complex. He begins with a response to Sanhedrin members who insist upon seeing His credentials.

In Jesus' day, the Sanhedrin was the supreme Jewish civil and religious authority. It consisted of Jewish officials representing the major religious sects and priesthood. Much like our three branches of government in the U.S. capital today, this group provided the secular and religious guidance for all Jewish matters.[4]

Jesus silences them by asking them to name the authority by which John the Baptist ministered. As they refused to answer, He implies that He and John share similar authority from God.

Next, the Pharisees and Herodians try to entrap the Lord by imposing religious legality of paying tribute (taxes) to Caesar (government). Jesus reminds them it is our civic duty to render to the government its due. However, one's civic duty should never conflict with one's spiritual obligation—rendering to God His due.[5]

Then, the Sadducees, who do not believe in a resurrection, pose a resurrection scenario. In the Lord's response, He affirms the resurrection and insists God is of the living, not the dead. In other words, there is eternal life beyond the grave.

The final challenge came from a pharisaic lawyer who asks Jesus to identify the greatest of God's commandments. He quotes from Deuteronomy 6:5 and Leviticus 19:18,

> "Love the Lord your God with all your heart and with all your soul and with all your mind." This is the first and greatest commandment. And the second is like it: "Love your neighbor as yourself." All the Law and the Prophets hang on these two commandments (Matthew 22:37–40 NIV).

With His final response, Jesus quiets and denounces His critics to the delight of the masses.

Before leaving the Temple, Jesus observes how people were putting their money offerings into the treasury; He calls His Disciples' attention to a poor widow who gives two coins (mites), which represented all she had. Then, He teaches on Jerusalem's forthcoming destruction in 70 AD, His glorious second coming, and of end-time events.

That same day, Jesus and His Disciples visit Simon the leper's home where Mary anoints Jesus' feet with costly ointment to the displeasure of Judas Iscariot. Jesus reprimands Judas for his outburst and assures everyone there her expression of love, gratitude, and worship would be remembered in perpetuity.

Later this same evening, motivated by anger, revenge, or greed, Judas contacts the Sanhedrin to arrange Jesus' betrayal for thirty pieces of silver.

Wednesday

This was an uneventful day in Bethany as Jesus agonizes over His beloved Jerusalem,

> O Jerusalem, Jerusalem, the city that kills the prophets and stones God's messengers! How often I have wanted to gather your children together as a hen protects her chicks beneath her wings, but you wouldn't let me (Luke 13:34 NLT).

Unbelievable Altruism

Thursday

The day of Unleavened Bread and the Passover Seder finally arrives requiring much preparation and fanfare,

> [The Passover Seder] consists of choice lamb roasted whole, unleavened bread, wine and bitter herbs. At sunset, the trumpets would blast, and the meal would begin. Before the sunset hour arrived, the Disciples would have completed all arrangements and would await the coming of Jesus. In due time, He arrived, and they were ready to celebrate this

memorial of the deliverance of their forefathers from Egyptian bondage.[6]

This evening fascinates me, as I wonder what the Lord was thinking and feeling. What were the Disciples thinking and feeling? There is a commentary on our Lord's contemplation that yet captivates my attention (*my emphasis*),

> You see, at just the right time, when we were still powerless, Christ died for the ungodly. *Very rarely* will anyone die for a righteous person, though for a good person someone might possibly dare to die. But, God demonstrates his own love for us in this: While we were still sinners, Christ died for us (Romans 5:6–8 NIV).

The first Adam's disobedience introduced sin into God's perfect world, which resulted in our spiritual and physical deaths. Our spiritual death (sin), which separates us from God, happened instantaneously while our physical death came gradually.

In essence, God created us to be holy (sinless) beings to live forever in His perfect world. But because of Adam's disobedience, our world is full of sadness, sin, pain, disease, trouble, and death. Thus as the Bible teaches, all of us will sin, and all of us will die (Romans 3:23, 5:14, 6:23).

In addition, since we are sinners by nature, our "good deeds" are sin-polluted.

A splendid illustration would be how when men wore white dress shirts and carrying a fountain pen in the shirt breast pocket was a common practice. Often, the ink pen leaked, and the slightest ink spot on the white shirt ruined the shirt—literally.

As the ink spot polluted the shirt, sin has polluted our righteousness. On our best day, we are still worthless before a holy God (who has never been polluted), and we fail before His righteousness as filthy rags,

> We are all infected and impure with sin. When we display our righteous deeds, they are nothing but filthy rags. Like autumn leaves, we wither and fall, and our sins sweep us away like the wind (Isaiah 64:6 NLT).

However, this is not the case with Jesus Christ. He was without sin and fully aware His death would redeem all fallen humanity from sin and restore us to a loving, eternal fellowship with God,

> Therefore, as through one man's offense judgment came to all men, resulting in condemnation, even so through one Man's righteous act the free gift came to all men, resulting in justification of life. For as by one man's disobedience many were made sinners, so also by one Man's obedience

many will be made righteous (Romans 5:18–19 NKJV).

It is truly unbelievable how Jesus freely chose to offer Himself to redeem the entire world—whether Jew, Gentile, rich, poor, believer or non-believer. All of us can vicariously receive the full benefit of His perfect sacrifice—without preference or distinction.

No longer do Satan, sin, and death bind us. From this day forward, our faith in His perfect, work determines our righteousness (or lack thereof) before our Heavenly Father.

Ultimately, Jesus chose to redeem those who love Him, those who hate Him, those who believe in Him, and those who do not believe in Him.

What a Wonderful Savior!

The idea of "equal atonement" is difficult for the modern mind to capture fully. Not concerning Christ's saving efficacy as His sacrifice remediates all our sins forever.

However, His commitment to give Himself freely and willingly for every man, woman, boy, and girl—past, present, and future—so comprehensively, is difficult to fathom. Such an action is not a normal human response, especially toward someone we feel is "less desirable."

Sacrificing for a loved one is conceivable when our love for them or our desire to protect them motivates us. However, choosing to sacrifice our lives for an enemy or someone who dislikes us is extremely hard to envision.

History has shown there may be certain situations where we would risk life and limb for someone we might not necessarily care for. During the Second World War, for example, cultural issues fostered adversarial relationships that fragmented our troops occasionally. Although these valiant men and women may have been divided, they proved themselves more than willing to sacrifice for their adversary's greater good by fighting and dying to spare the world from the global tyranny of the Axis powers.

Fast-forward eighty years to our current global pandemic. We have replaced our noble altruism with a cold-hearted malevolence as we maliciously engage in "germ warfare" by unleashing a virus that targets innocent victims with underlying health issues around the world. Then, we withhold vital technologies and politicize medical remedies that can prevent and treat illness and improve our overall health and safety. Finally, we hoard or resell safety supplies at inflated prices and expose those who are vulnerable, with premorbidities to even more danger.

I am saddened by the barbarism plaguing human hearts today. Truly, the Enemy is at work in the callous and malicious disregard for human dignity witnessed in the indiscriminate killing of the unborn and helpless, the calculated euthanization of the weak and aged, and the exploitation, abuse, trafficking, oppression, and violence perpetrated against all those who fall between these two extremes. Ultimately, we have reduced precious, God-given lives to mere dollars and cents.

Our heartlessness is most unfortunate because technology, education, politics, military, and industry do not make our country great. It is our faith in God, and the Judeo-Christian values we embrace and uphold, as the Scriptures attest, "Righteousness exalts a nation, but sin is a reproach to any people" (Proverbs 14:34 NKJV).

Ours is not a perfect nation; no nation is, especially with sin and entitlement issues running amuck as they are today. Nevertheless, there was a time in our not-too-distant past when we understood right from wrong, and we intuitively maintained a line of demarcation between what was morally good and morally bad.

Unfortunately, we have erased that line by our existential relativism. Our existentialism celebrates our human subjectivity while our relativism denies the existence of all absolute truth,

> Dress as you will, fornicate with whom you will, infect whom you will, wear clothes, or go naked as you will. The only right is what is right for you, and the only

wrong is that which produces pain or inconvenience for you. There is no law, no principle, no proper course of action of any kind, so go with the vibes! Whatever is your thing, do it.[7]

God's Word (Bible) and His Helper (Holy Spirit) no longer guide our thoughts, words, and behavior. Instead, whatever feels good or gives us pleasure—*at this moment*—is what governs our conscience and behavior.

Oh, what sorrow and despair await those of us who insist "evil is good and good is evil, that dark is light and light is dark, that bitter is sweet and sweet is bitter" (Isaiah 5:20 NLT).

A civilized people must exercise vigilance and due diligence to promote and secure the moral and spiritual well-being of our fellow countrymen and women,

> The freedom of God is exercised and illustrated in His government of His moral creatures. It has pleased God to create intelligences possessed of moral freedom and to make their ultimate destiny contingent upon the right use of their freedom.[8]

God has endowed all of us with the sacred trust to preserve civility, decency, and goodwill for people with whom we work, serve, and live.

Those of us over twenty-one years of age especially should be fostering a congenial atmosphere since we have matured beyond our childish self-interests to pursue those things that are in everyone's collective best interest. We who have so matured understand if we persist in raucous discord, no person will be spared from hostility and violence.

At some point, we must pause to ask this question with the utmost sincerity, *what kind of world do we want for our children, and their children?*

Therefore, with our non-absolute, selfish, proud, twenty-first-century minds, it is extremely difficult to imagine how someone in perfect health, with all His faculties, and less than twenty-four hours to live would spend His remaining moments teaching enduring lessons that would shape future generations of His Followers around the world as Jesus did on His last evening.

In His shoes, we would spend our last moments fulfilling selfish desires, visiting exotic places, visit our families and close friends, or completing unfinished tasks on our "bucket list."

Not so with Jesus Christ. He knew He would die on the cross shortly, and He spent His remaining moments with His beloved Disciples, sharing lessons most important to them (and us).

Jesus begins with some object lessons for new living. We will explore them in the next chapter.

Notes

[1] The original name: Abib (Exodus 13:4) was changed to Nisan after Israel's exile from Babylonian captivity (Nehemiah 2:1 and Esther 3:7).

[2] Ceil and Moishe Rosen, *Christ in the Passover: Why is this Night Different*, 6th ed., (Chicago: Moody, 1980) 42.

[3] The Passover and Feast of Unleavened Bread occur between our March and April; the Feast of Weeks or Pentecost occurs between our May and June, and the Feast of Booths or Tabernacles occurs between our September and October.

[4] H. E. Dana, "Sanhedrin," *The New Testament World*, rev. 3rd ed., (Nashville: Broadman, 1937) 115–116.

[5] Civic obligations should never preclude our lawful, religious obligations. When government sanctions oppose lawful matters of faith and practice, then our appropriate response becomes a matter of Scripture and conscience.

[6] H. I. Hester, *The Heart of the New Testament*, 35th ed., (Nashville: Broadman Press, 1981) 197.

[7] For further discussion, see: Dave Breese, *Seven Men Who Rule the World from the Grave*, (Chicago: Moody Press, 1990) 217, and William L. Reese, "Existentialism," *Dictionary of Philosophy and Religion: Eastern and Western Thought*, 8th ed., (Atlantic Highlands, NJ: Humanities Press, 1980) 163–164, and "Relativism," 487.

[8] Merrill F. Unger, "Freedom," *Unger's Bible Dictionary*, 18th printing, (Chicago: Moody Press, 1972) 380.

Chapter Two

Chapter Two:
Presenting A New Covenant

A Lesson on Humility

In Jesus' day, people did not have access to the many forms of motorized transportation (i.e., motorcycles, cars, trucks, trains, airplanes, etc.) we have today. In addition, the roads were not paved. So depending on the terrain and weather conditions, travel could be extremely messy.

People who could not afford to ride animals (i.e., camels, donkeys, horses, etc.) walked, exposing their sandaled feet to dirty roads—sometimes checkered with animal feces. Thus, as a common courtesy (and sanitary reasons), the host provided for foot washing since the guest's feet were soiled by the time they reached their destination.

Also in Jesus' day and culture, people ate while reclining on one side—sometimes with their feet extended toward other guests,

> Reclining on the triclinium, or dinner bed, the guest lay usually upon his left side, leaving his right hand free to reach for food. His head would thus easily come into contact with the breast of the person on his left. It was in this way that John leaned on the bosom of Jesus while at supper.[1]

Foot washing was the task reserved for the lowest ranking person (or servant) in the household. However, in this instance, Jesus "flipped the script" by washing the Twelve Disciples' feet as if He was the lowest ranking servant. In so doing, He teaches an unmistakable object lesson on humility to the astonishment of His Disciples,

> It was at this juncture that Jesus washed the feet of the Disciples. It was an object lesson to impress upon them the quality of true greatness. He was their Lord, and yet He became their servant as He laid aside His garments, took a towel and girded Himself, poured water into a basin, and stooped to wash the feet of His Disciples. Jesus was not instituting an ordinance like that of the Lord's Supper but was giving an object lesson in true humility of spirit.[2]

The Lord exercises great patience with His Disciples' failure to understand the importance of humility and selflessness. He was their Rabbi (leader and teacher), yet He lowered Himself to serve them when it was their obligation to serve Him. (To the Disciples' credit, there was no designated servant present to wash their feet since the gathering was a private one.)

The Disciples also failed to grasp the vast spiritual dimension of the Kingdom of God where our Lord reigns forever in full majesty and glory. (They were too busy arguing about who would be "greatest" in the Kingdom and forgot that someone within their ranks should have performed the task.)

Jesus teaches His Disciples what constitutes true greatness—*humility*—especially for His people. His actions were consistent with His earlier teachings, "If any man will come after me, let him deny himself, and take up his cross, and follow me" (Matthew 16:24 AKJV).

Jesus was the ultimate example of humility as He relinquished His deity and took on human form to pay for our sin,

> Though he was God, he did not think of equality with God as something to cling to. Instead, he gave up his divine privileges; he took the humble position of a slave and was born as a human being. When he appeared in human form, he humbled himself in obedience to God and died a criminal's death on a cross (Philippians 2:6–8 NLT).

As the Passover Seder resumes, Jesus identifies Judas as the traitor. Then, Judas leaves the gathering to arrange the betrayal with the Sanhedrin.

With the traitor now gone, there is a distinctive change in the atmosphere. Jesus elevates His teachings to speak candidly on enduring faith lessons that they would present to the entire world in about fifty days, the Day of Pentecost.

A New Commandment

Earlier in the week, Jesus tells how the greatest commandment is to love God and our neighbors as ourselves. Now He adds a new wrinkle; *love as I love you,*

> A new commandment I give to you, that you love one another; as I have loved you, that you also love one another. By this all will know that you are My disciples, if you have love for one another (John 13:34–35 NKJV).

In this context, Jesus uses the verb form of the Greek word for love, *agapao* (Strong-G25), to describe the act of affection or benevolence directed toward another family member.[3]

In so doing, our Lord institutes a "love mandate" for His people who will carry on His work. This will be in stark contrast to the world—a cold, cruel, and lonely place where smiles are rare, and people are too pre-occupied with themselves to establish and preserve lasting relationships.

Our world will never produce the unifying, loving message Christ gives His people. Jesus' new love paradigm ensures that *His* love will always be the guiding principle for every Follower of Christ, which contradicts the prejudice and intolerance our world accepts and embraces.

As brothers and sisters in Christ, we are a unified community of faith and peace serving one God,

> Endeavoring to keep the unity of the Spirit in the bond of peace. There is one body and one Spirit, just as you were called in one hope of your calling; one Lord, one faith, one baptism; one God and Father of all, who is above all, and through all, and in you all (Ephesians 4:3–6 NKJV).

We share the same Lord who makes us one, as He is one with His Father. We are joint heirs of His undeserved grace, because He shed His blood for all of us, individually and collectively (Romans 8:17).

Because He loves and forgives us, we can love and forgive each other as we unite in Christ. His Spirit within us urges and empowers us to demonstrate His love with unmistakable fervor.

We may not share doctrine or liturgy; we may not share race, culture, or language, yet we are comfortable around each other. Expressing our affection is made possible because we love, just as He loves us.

The Greek word to describe our loving fellowship is *koinonia* (Strong-G2842), where we fellowship, share, participate, and commune together as the Bible teaches,[4]

> We have fellowship with each other, and the blood of Jesus, his Son, cleanses us from all sin (1 John 1:7 NLT).

The miracle of diverse unity under the banner of Christ validates His distinctive message of transformation, acceptance, and renewal as we share meals, celebrate special occasions, and attend gatherings where there are no outcasts.

Most importantly, we reveal it is possible for diverse people to coexist peacefully. This distinct Christian witness verifies our association with Christ where His love prevails and makes us one,

> The Israelite had been charged to love his neighbor as himself (Leviticus 19:19), so the command of Jesus was not new in every respect. But it had a new frame of reference, as fellow believer now takes the place of neighbor, not in the sense of supplanting the old obligation, but rather of extending it to all who share the faith. By limiting the sphere to believers, Jesus is not excluding love for all men but is simply stressing what must prevail among His followers.[5]

In practical terms, we treat our brothers and sisters in Christ with the utmost respect and acceptance demonstrating characteristics featured in the "Love Chapter" (1 Corinthians 13).

Patient and kind, we are not jealous, boastful, proud, or rude. We are not possessive and irritable, we make no demands, keep no record of wrongs, and we do not rejoice when wicked triumphs. We rejoice in truth, bear all things, believe all things, hope all things, and endure all things together.

We share a concern for all Christians because as one of us suffers, we all suffer. Our love is not abstract. It is practical as we focus on what unites us rather than on the petty issues that can divide us. Our union with Christ is unbreakable, and with it, He works through us to fulfill His new standard phenomenally.

In Remembrance of Me

As our Lord resumes the Passover Seder, He self-authenticates His New Covenant for us,

> The Lord Jesus, on the night he was betrayed, took bread, and when he had given thanks, he broke it and said, "This is my body, which is for you; do this in remembrance of me." In the same way, after supper he took the cup, saying, "This cup is the new covenant in my blood; do this, whenever you drink it, in remembrance of me." For whenever you eat this bread and drink this cup, you

proclaim the Lord's death until he comes (1 Corinthians 11:23–26 NIV).

In this intimate gathering, Jesus institutes a solemn memorial of His passion and death that features His body and blood, the Lord's Supper,

> At this stage of the [Passover] meal, its character had suddenly been changed. The Old Covenant (or Testament) Passover became, by an act of Jesus, a New Covenant (or Testament) supper. He told His Disciples that the bread was His body "given" for them, and the cup was the New Covenant or Testament in His blood. Then, He told them that whenever they should meet together for a meal after His departure, they should remember how He had given His whole life for them.[6]

"In remembrance of me" implies we publicly and regularly observe the Lord's death to remind ourselves of His redeeming work. We do not perform this act callously or frivolously. Instead, we solemnly partake these two elements; bread to symbolize our Lord's body offered on Calvary's cross as our sacrifice and the wine to symbolize the blood He shed to remediate our sin.

His sacrifice was necessary. Adam and Eve's original disobedience in the Garden of Eden has subjected us to God's judgment. We are sinners by hereditary transmission and can never earn God's favor on our merit.

Only God is just, right, and holy while we are not. His justice demands payment for sin, and His righteousness requires our total obedience to His standards (the Law). His holiness necessitates our utter perfection—in every aspect of our being.

The payment for sin is death. Jesus speaks of death, encompassing our banishment to a fiery Hell where worms never die and where tormenting fires burn forever (Mark 9:48).

Initially, God instructed Moses to use a sacrificial offering to remediate our sin,

> For the life of the flesh is in the blood, and I have given it to you upon the altar to make atonement for your souls; for it is the blood that makes atonement for the soul (Leviticus 17:11 NKJV).

Although God gave instructions to use a "clean" animal's blood to cover sin, it was not a permanent fix since we had to repeat the process.

Instead, it foreshadowed the restitution Christ would provide to completely wash away our sins, make us righteous, and restore our lost fellowship with God,

> For you know that it was not with perishable things such as silver or gold

that you were redeemed, but with the precious blood of Christ, a lamb without blemish or defect (1 Peter 1:18–19 NIV)

Through the Lord's Supper, we demonstrate our faith in Jesus Christ, the Bread of Life, who paid the full price for our sin. We also show that in Him, we find our dependence on Him for our spiritual life and vitality.

Further, we show our hope of eternal life through His resurrection from the dead. The Lord commands us to eat and drink of the Lord's Supper until He eats and drinks it with us anew in the Kingdom of God.

Now, Jesus begins teaching about our future home, His identity, His replacement, and our peace. We will explore these lessons in the next chapter.

Notes

[1] James M. Freeman, "Position at Table," *Manners and Customs of the Bible*, reprint, (Plainfield: Logos International, 1972) 432.

[2] H. I. Hester, *The Heart of the New Testament*, 35th ed., (Nashville: Broadman Press, 1981) 197.

[3] Walter Bauer, "ἀγαπάω," *A Greek-English Lexicon of the New Testament and Other Early Christian Literature* , ed., F. Wilbur Gingrich and Frederick W. Danker, 2nd rev. ed. (Chicago: University of Chicago Press, 1979) 4, and James Strong, "ἀγαπάω," "Dictionary of Greek Words," *Strong's Exhaustive Concordance of the Bible*, updated ed., 3rd printing, (Peabody: Hendrickson Publishers, 2009) 1599.

[4] Spiros Zodhiates, "κοινωνία," *The Complete Word Study Dictionary, New Testament*, rev. ed., (Chattanooga: AMG International, 1993) 873, and W.E. Vine, "Fellowship," *An Expository Dictionary of New Testament Words*, in *Vine's Expository Dictionary of Biblical Words*, rev. ed. (Nashville: Thomas Nelson, 1985) 233.

[5] Everett F. Harrison, *A Short Life of Christ*, reprint, (Grand Rapids: Wm. B. Eerdmans Publishing Company, 2001) 182.

[6] Ray F. Robbins, *The Life and Ministry of Our Lord*, (Nashville: Convention Press, 1970) 144.

Chapter Three

Chapter Three:
One Distinct Person and Plan

Let Not Your Heart be Troubled

 The Disciples were deeply troubled after the Lord announces His departure, Peter's denials, and their future abandonment.

For three and a half years, they spent every waking moment together. Now, they would no longer be with their blessed Lord. The Disciples pondered how they would survive without the Lord's guidance indefinitely.

Having established that His loving community will serve each other, practice humility, and gather regularly to remember Him, Jesus now comforts them (and us) by telling how He will be preparing our eternal dwelling place,

> Do not let your hearts be troubled. You believe in God; believe also in me. My Father's house has many rooms; if that were not so, would I have told you that I am going there to prepare a place for you? And if I go and prepare a place for you, I will come back and take you to be with me that you also may be where I am (John 14:1–3 NIV).

Jesus inspires us to have faith in Him and God—a solid foundation that secures all our future hopes and desires.

Christ is no longer with us physically. He has gone to His Father. Our journey is now a "faith walk" that looks back to the cross and forward to vast, unimaginable treasures He is preparing for us in His Father's house.

Our hearts cease from being troubled whenever we seek and anticipate the magnificent, spiritual blessings not visible to the world that await us,

> So we fix our eyes not on what is seen, but on what is unseen, since what is seen is temporary, but what is unseen is eternal (2 Corinthians 4:18 NIV).

Our chief aim is to occupy our glorious, heavenly home, where "the wicked shall cease from troubling, and the weary shall be at rest" (Job 3:17). The hopes and desires of all Believers everywhere are found in this central expectation—to occupy Heaven with Christ and God.

There we have perfect understanding of the work and ways of God. We no longer "know in part" but will know Him as we are known by Him, and we will "see Him as He is" in His full majestic splendor (1 Corinthians 13:9, 1 John 3:2).

Jesus is preparing a place where holiness, glory, peace, harmony, love, rest, and unspeakable joy abound beyond our most vivid imagination. Our eternal home (*glorification*) is where we will bask in God's full, unfiltered presence without sin, pain, or disease,

> So when this corruptible shall have put on incorruption, and this mortal shall have put on immortality, then shall be brought to pass the saying that is written, death is swallowed up in victory (1 Corinthians 15:54 AKJV).

It is a place where He will "wipe away all tears from our eyes" as we are blessed and satisfied beyond anything we have seen or heard here on earth (Revelation 21:4). We are truly blessed forever,

> Blessed are the dead who die in the Lord from now on…They will rest from their labor, for their deeds will follow them (Revelation 14:13 NIV).

Standing on the observation deck at the Grand Canyon can be a breath-taking experience, as is Niagara Falls, where one can hear and feel its sheer power and massive volume. In addition, stately Redwoods, white, sandy, tropical beaches, beautiful ocean sunrises, or sunsets filled with striking pastel colors are most memorable earthly experiences as well.

Nevertheless, none of these moving experiences can compare to a split-second in our eternal home,

> No eye has seen, no ear has heard, and no mind has imagined what God has prepared for those who love him (1 Corinthians 2:9 NLT).

This earth is not our home. We are pilgrims passing through it briefly. Thus, God gave us a yearning spiritual dimension that craves to be with Him. The "whole earth groans" as we anxiously await His glorious return. Then we, along with those who have died in the Lord, will be reunited (Romans 8:22, 1 Thessalonians 4:13–18). Until then, our comfort is in knowing we will see Him again, coming in the clouds with great power and glory (Mark 13:26).

Yet, our Christian faith is more than a "pie-in-the-sky" religion filled with future promises. Ours is a faith that produces a life of abundance (John 10:10) that starts from the time we accept Christ as our Savior and Lord, and it continues throughout eternity.

Having our sins forgiven and peace with God makes our faith more precious than anything on earth. Yet, as we continue this Christian journey, we have considerably more treasures to receive.

Those who refuse to acknowledge Jesus Christ as Lord and Savior in this life meet Him as Eternal Judge in the next. However, we who love Him and have faith that begins and ends with Him know

He is our hope, peace, and our wonderful, eternal reward.

The Way, Truth, and Life

When Thomas tells the Lord the Disciples do not know where He is going or how they could get there, Jesus responds with an unforgettable lesson on His uniquely transcendent person,

> I am the way, the truth, and the life. No one comes to the Father except through Me (John 14:6 NKJV).

The Greek word for way, *hodos* (Strong-G3598), is used to distinguish something from the normal path or way.[1]

This is most significant, as the world would refer to Believers as followers of "the way" (Acts 9:2). Jesus' characterization of Himself was intentional and emphatically clear. He is the *only* way to the Father,

> I do not merely point out the way, teach the truth, and bestow life, but I am the way, the truth, and the life, so that by attachment to Me, one necessarily is in the way and possesses the truth and the life. He is the goal of all human aspiration.[2]

Jesus also speaks in deistic terms, as though He is God, the ultimate authority, ensuring our access to the Father,

> Christ is the gate. He is the way. There is no other avenue to Heaven. Every other choice is wrong. There is no in between, no third alternative, no other gate. The options are simple and straightforward. There are not many good religions; there is only one. And so the options are only two—the true and the false, the right and the wrong, God's way and humankind's way. All this world's religions are based on human achievement. Biblical Christianity alone recognizes divine accomplishment—the work of Christ on humankind's behalf—as the sole basis of salvation.[3]

Peter repeats Jesus' distinctive tone when he addresses the religious leaders shortly thereafter,

> Jesus is the stone you builders rejected, which has become the cornerstone. Salvation is found in no one else, for there is no other name under heaven given to mankind by which we must be saved (Acts 4:11–12 NIV).

Not only is Jesus the way, but He is also the embodiment of absolute truth. The Greek word used for truth here is *aletheia* (Strong-G225), which differentiates something from a mere object of knowledge or intellectual inquiry.[4]

In other words, Jesus is not some common source of moral and ethical truth. He is "truth in all its fullness and scope." He is the perfect expression of any-and-all truth—past, present, and future.

When Pontius Pilate sarcastically retorted, "What is truth?" (John 18:38), he had no idea of the vast implications of his remark. He was oblivious to speaking with Jesus Christ—truth personified.

As we consider His life, teachings, death, and resurrection objectively, His uniqueness as our only God and Savior becomes unmistakably clear. God is the source of truth, and Jesus Christ is His representation of all that is true—in all its straightforwardness and complete authenticity.

Not just the way and truth, Jesus is the source of abundant and everlasting life. His words, "I am the resurrection and the life" (John 11:25), are consistent with His pre-incarnate being,

> He was with God in the beginning. Through him all things were made; without Him nothing was made that has been made. In him was life, and that life was the light of all mankind. The light shines in the darkness, and the darkness has not overcome it (John 1:2–5 NIV).

The Greek word used for life is *zoe* (Strong-G2222), to describe physical and spiritual life, which finds their origin and continuance in God, who is the source of all life.[5]

Only the Lord can bestow life that becomes the "light to all mankind;" a rich, fulfilling life to all who place their trust in Him. Because of Him, we live, move, and have our being (Acts 17:28).

Jesus is not one who merely points the way to God or shows us how we can know God intellectually. He is God in human flesh so that when we see Him, we see the Father (John 14:9).

Since He and the Father are one, He offers the means to restore our broken fellowship with God. Only then can we experience God personally, intimately, and profoundly in ways that affect substantive spiritual changes that last forever.

Jesus Christ left glory, not because of what we could do for Him, but because of what He could do for us—provide the way to God. He performed this wonderful work because He loves us more than we could ever comprehend. It is not our works but our faith in His works that allows us to return to God.

Because of His perfect work, we can be fully confident that God will hear and answer us when we can pray *in Jesus' name*. Jesus' perfect merit guarantees the Father's immediate attention.

The Helper Is on the Way

The Lord then tells how certain dramatic spiritual changes will verify our union with Him as well as the condition of our hearts toward Him,

> If you love Me, keep My commandments. And I will pray the Father, and He will give you another Helper, that He may abide with you forever—the Spirit of truth, whom the world cannot receive, because it neither sees Him nor knows Him; but you know Him, for He dwells with you and will be in you. I will not leave you orphans; I will come to you…But the Helper, the Holy Spirit, whom the Father will send in My name, He will teach you all things, and bring to your remembrance all things that I said to you (John 14:15-18, 26 NKJV).

Jesus' Followers will love Him and adhere to His commandments. Thus, His standards for moral and spiritual living are not for our selective "picking and choosing." We obey them because we love Him and desire to please Him.

In His human form, Jesus could not be in more than one place at one time. The Helper ensures that everyone can experience the fullness of Christ around the world simultaneously,

> [The Helper] makes it possible for Him to be united to, and to be present in each Believer, as perfectly and fully as if that Believer were the only one to receive

Christ's fullness. Each Believer has the whole Christ with him as his source of strength, purity, life; so that each may say: Christ gives all His time and wisdom and care to me. Such a union as this lacks every element of instability. Once formed, the union is indissoluble. Many of the ties of earth are rudely broken—not so with our union with Christ—that endures forever. Since there is now an unchangeable and divine element in us, our salvation depends no longer upon our unstable wills, but upon Christ's purpose and power.[6]

Parakleteos (Strong-G3875) is the Greek word for our Helper and Advocate. It combines two Greek words, *para* (Strong-G3844) and *kaleo* (Strong-2564). Para means to "come alongside," and kaleo means to "call or summon."[7]

The Helper comes alongside to be our duly appointed representative of Jesus Christ. Only He can fulfill all the rights, privileges, and responsibilities appertaining thereto.

As our Comforter, He "seals" our reclamation to secure our heavenly home (Ephesians 4:30). Here, He keeps our thoughts and desires focused on yesterday's redemption, today's salvation, and tomorrow's bliss through Christ.

As our Advocate, He is our perfect guide to give us direction, purpose, and meaning as Almighty

God in Spirit. As the Holy Spirit, He purifies, strengthens, encourages, reveals, and keeps us forever.

He is also our Teacher, who brings to our minds those precious and unforgettable teachings that reinforce how wonderful our Lord continues to be,

> Come to me, all of you who are weary and carry heavy burdens, and I will give you rest. Take my yoke upon you. Let me teach you, because I am humble and gentle at heart, and you will find rest for your souls. For my yoke is easy to bear, and the burden I give you is light (Matthew 11:28–30 NLT).

The Holy Spirit has not for the world, but for Followers of Christ exclusively. He cannot live inside those who reject God's love and forgiveness through Christ. Sin-skewed, temporal minds will never appreciate our Lord's presence, power, and wonderful spiritual blessings (1 Corinthians 2:14).

My Peace I Leave with You

Through Jesus Christ, we have been reconciled to God and can have peace with Him forever,

> [Peace with God] expresses the state of reconciliation. Sin is the source of all discord and war between man and God, and between man and man; and hence there can be no peace until this curse is

removed. All other peace is an idle dream and illusion. Being at peace with God, we are at peace with ourselves and with our fellow men.[8]

Our peace with God is complete and eternal. We have been accepted into His holy and righteous presence and are no longer at odds with Him due to our sinful past. Jesus says He will not repel anyone who comes to Him by faith (John 6:37).

Peace translates into a clear conscience that frees us from our sinful past and opens new future opportunities beyond our wildest dreams.

The Helper provides us with peace and tranquility to dispel our anxieties and fears so that even when we face turmoil, that when we take rest, our sleep is sweet (Proverbs 3:24).

The Helper replaces our worries, anxieties, and fears with His calm, assurance, and ease as we concentrate on the Lord,

> You will keep him in perfect peace, Whose mind is stayed on You, Because he trusts in You (Isaiah 26:3 NKJV).

Adversity, difficulty, and temptation do not devastate us because the Helper is in us to sustain us. God is faithful, and He has promised not to allow anything to overwhelm us,

> God is faithful. He will not allow the temptation to be more than you can stand. When you are tempted, he will show you a way out so that you can endure (1 Corinthians 10:13 NLT).

With His peace, we can be peaceful toward others by not expressing ill will. The Lord sees all our works, both good and bad, and He will avenge accordingly (Deuteronomy 32:35, Romans 12:19).

Ours is a perfect peace that will last forever. It is not attached to circumstances but subject to His sustaining work in us. Herein is our source of optimal comfort,

> Rejoice in the Lord always. I will say it again: Rejoice!...Do not be anxious about anything, but in every situation, by prayer and petition, with thanksgiving, present your requests to God. And the peace of God, which transcends all understanding, will guard your hearts and your minds in Christ Jesus. Finally, brothers and sisters, whatever is true, whatever is noble, whatever is right, whatever is pure, whatever is lovely, whatever is admirable—if anything is excellent or praiseworthy—think about such things...And the God of peace will be with you (Philippians 4:4, 6–9 NIV).

Our past is immaterial since it has been nailed to the cross (Colossians 2:14). We stand, totally reconciled by the blood of Jesus Christ. We were once enemies, but now we are at peace with Him. This is God's grace, and it is truly amazing.

Leaving the upper room and the Passover Seder, Jesus walks with His Disciples to Gethsemane. As they walk, the Lord teaches valuable lessons and reassures them He will not abandon them, but will abide with them and us forever.

We will explore these lessons in the next chapter.

Notes

[1] Walter Bauer, "ὁδός," *A Greek-English Lexicon of the New Testament and Other Early Christian Literature*, ed., F. Wilbur Gingrich and Frederick W. Danker, 2nd rev. ed. (Chicago: University of Chicago Press, 1979) 553–555, and W.E. Vine, "Way," *An Expository Dictionary of New Testament Words*, in *Vine's Expository Dictionary of Biblical Words*, rev. ed. (Nashville: Thomas Nelson, 1985) 668–669.

[2] Marcus Dods, "The Synoptic Gospel of St. John," *The Expositor's Greek New Testament*, reprint, ed., Robertson Nicholl, vol. 1, (Grand Rapids: Wm. B. Eerdmans, 1980) 822.

[3] John F. MacArthur, Jr., *The Gospel According To Jesus*, revised & expanded, (Grand Rapids: Zondervan Publishing House, 1994) 205.

[4] Walter Bauer, "ἀλήθεια," 35–36, W.E. Vine, "True, Truly, Truth," 245, and William L. Reese, "Truth," *Dictionary of Philosophy and Religion: Eastern and Western Thought*, 8th ed., (Atlantic Highlands: Humanities Press, 1991) 588.

[5] Walter Bauer, "ζωή," 340–341.

[6] Augustus H. Strong, *Systematic Theology*, 31st ed., (Valley Forge: Judson Press, 1976) 801.

[7] Spiros Zodhiates, "παράκλητος," *The Complete Word Study Dictionary, New Testament*, rev. ed., (Chattanooga: AMG International, 1993) 1107 & 1105.

[8] J.P. Lange, and F.R. Fay, "The Epistle of Paul to the Romans," *Commentary on the Holy Scriptures: Critical, Doctrinal and Homiletical*, trans., J.F. Hurst, P. Schaff and M.B. Riddle, 7th ed., vol. 10, (Grand Rapids: Zondervan, 1980) 160.

Chapter Four

Chapter Four:
True Vine's Chosen Ones

I Am the Vine—You are the Branches

 The Disciples' levels of perplexity, anxiety, and uncertainty must have been extreme as the Lord spoke that evening on their way to Gethsemane.

Keep in mind, Jesus was fully aware of Judas' plot to betray Him, the Disciples' abandonment and denials, the religious leaders' disgraceful, mock trial, and His humiliating public execution. However, the Disciples were not. They were oblivious to these events and feeling bewildered.

They just heard the Lord tell them He was leaving and later returning to them. They heard about the coming Helper, but they did not know how or when He would arrive. They had no idea what would become of their faith movement after Jesus' departure, or who would lead it.

Now, the Lord uses metaphorical language that must have seemed even more baffling,

> I am the true vine, and My Father is the vinedresser. Every branch in Me that does not bear fruit He takes away; and every branch that bears fruit He prunes, that it may bear more fruit. You are already clean because of the word which I have

spoken to you. Abide in Me, and I in you. As the branch cannot bear fruit of itself, unless it abides in the vine, neither can you, unless you abide in Me. "I am the vine, you are the branches. He who abides in Me, and I in him, bears much fruit; for without Me you can do nothing" (John 15:1–5 NKJV).

Jesus identifies Himself as the *True Vine*, the authentic and legitimate "real deal." Before Him, were imitators, and after Him, pretenders.

He is the stalk, and we are fruit-producing branches proceeding from Him. We are rooted in Him, and without Him, we will wither and die.

Jesus alone is the source of our life and purpose. Because of our association, we can have access to all the spiritual, life-giving resources He has at His disposal.

In other words, He alone is the object of our faith, the essence of our spiritual life, and the realization of all our future hopes and desires,

> As God's natural life is in the vine, Christ, that He may give life to His spiritual branches. The roots of this new vine are planted in Heaven, not on earth; and unto it, the half-withered branches of the old humanity are to be grafted, that they may have life divine. Our Lord does not say, "I am the root." The branch is not something

outside, which has to get nourishment out of the root. It is rather a part of the vine. Not only grounded in Christ as our foundation, but thrusting down root into Him as the deep, rich, all-sustaining soil.[1]

Abiding in the True Vine necessitates our complete surrender so that the Helper inside us can foster our consecrated, Christ-likeness,

> My old self has been crucified with Christ. It is no longer I who live, but Christ lives in me. So I live in this earthly body by trusting in the Son of God, who loved me and gave himself for me (Galatians 2:20 NLT).

Crucified with Christ may seem odd, but it is not. Christ is our identity; we draw our strength from Him. He is our life and power to perform godly activities that honor Him; activities our old nature protests and resists—vehemently.

Our Father's pruning is therefore required for fruit-bearing. The Greek word for pruning is *kathairo* (Strong-G2508), to cut away the undesirable and unfruitful parts, to cleanse from filth, to prune or eliminate that which is fruitless, or to purify.[2]

We face no condemnation in Christ as we walk and live surrendered to His Spirit, our Helper (Romans 8:1). Our purging is of the Father in the whole process of our "removing temptations and afflictions."[3] This is our sanctification.

As we walk in His Spirit, the Helper enables us to experience the "power of Jesus' resurrection" and "fellowship in the Lord's suffering;" to mortify the flesh so as to conform to His righteousness in living (Philippians 3:10).

We bear fruit by striving toward spiritual perfection through fasting,[4] prayer, reading and studying God's Word (Bible), attending church regularly, and Christian service.

Ultimately, as we yield, the Helper will conform us into the image and likeness of Christ. This was true for the Disciples then, and it is true for us today.

Conformed to Christ's Image and Likeness

God commands His people to be holy, and Jesus says we are to be perfect (Leviticus 20:26, Matthew 5:48). Thus, the Helper abides with us and in us, sanctifying our thoughts, words, and actions into Christ's likeness,

> That in this conflict the Holy Spirit enables the Christian, through increasing faith, more fully and consciously to appropriate Christ, and thus progressively to make a conquest of the remaining sinfulness of his nature.[5]

The Helper will not conform us to worldly standards. Instead, He renews our minds and transforms us so that we can reveal God's good, acceptable, and perfect will (Romans 12:2).

With our renewed, willing mind, our Helper also implants a growing fervor in us for godly things. Simultaneously, He also fosters a progressive distaste for worldly things that stunt our spiritual growth and hinder our intimate and vital connection with the True Vine.

The fruit we bear is not to achieve our salvation. The Helper living inside us prompts us to make godly, moral choices, and to perform selfless, noble acts consistently—*because we are saved*.

Although we grow in our trust, surrender, and service, we will never achieve perfection in this life. Only Jesus was perfect. When we fail, we grieve the Helper, who desires "the best" outcome for us, which has never been sin (Ephesians 4:30).

On those occasions when we walk in pride, selfishness, lust, or spite, the Helper supplies us with the power we need to resist making excuses to mask our sin. He urges us to "come clean" by repenting to God and reconciling with the person or people we've offended.

Then, we can resume our spiritual journey with a greater determination to live for Christ and not for ourselves. The Helper also strengthens our resolve and ability not to repeat those same offenses.

Imperfection does not signal our defeat. It only reminds us how far we are from Christ's perfection and how important it is to rely on the Helper for our spiritual growth and development.

It is only the Holy Spirit of Christ—our perfect example—who can empower us to live consecrated, Christ-centered, and God-honoring lives that diametrically oppose our former life of sin. Over time, He will break our bonds of addiction and compulsive disorders, as we surrender more of ourselves to Him completely.

Our sanctification requires our constant vigilance and commitment until the day He returns and reigns supreme, and we are made perfect in Him,

> Since, then, you have been raised with Christ, set your hearts on things above, where Christ is, seated at the right hand of God. Set your minds on things above, not on earthly things. For you died, and your life is now hidden with Christ in God. When Christ, who is your life, appears, then you also will appear with him in glory (Colossians 3:1–4 NIV).

Our utter and absolute dependence is on the Vine to accomplish through us His perfect will for all those we will encounter daily. It is not our "power or might." Instead, it is the Helper in us, who makes all the difference in this our compelling lifestyle and witness (Zechariah 4:6).

I Have Chosen You

As Jesus abides in and obeys His Father, we abide in Him and obey Him. Our association with Christ elevates us beyond the status of mere servants to specifically chosen and divinely appointed friends,

> You are my friends if you do what I command. I no longer call you servants, because a servant does not know his master's business. Instead, I have called you friends, for everything that I learned from my Father I have made known to you. You did not choose me, but I chose you and appointed you so that you might go and bear fruit—fruit that will last—and so that whatever you ask in my name the Father will give you (John 15:14-16 NIV).

Jesus removes all social barriers by bestowing the title "friend." The Greek word used here is *philos* (Strong-G5384),[6] which denotes a dearly beloved, highly personal, trusted friend or companion, and it can be translated as brother. It is as if Jesus is saying to us,

> I have admitted you in to a state of the most intimate fellowship with myself; and have made known unto you whatsoever I have heard from the Father.[7]

Jesus raises His Followers to a permanent station of dignity and value. God proved His love and value for us by offering the best He had to redeem us forever.

We no longer carry the title of "servant" exclusively, although we surrender and obey Him to show our allegiance and practice humility, acknowledging His Lordship as the Firstborn of His people (Romans 8:29).

We are now friends, who can expect to receive all the gifts and graces He promises as our true Friend, who is closer than siblings are (Proverbs 18:24). Our Friend is loyal and caring. He is faithful and dependable. He is there to defend us, He keeps His promises, and He accompanies us everywhere we go. *He is our best Friend!*

Jesus teaches His Disciples that together as friends, all of us have an unbreakable bond as brothers and sisters in Christ with God as our Father. Together, we share these spiritual gifts and graces He provides in conjunction with the Helper's sanctifying work within us.

We Are Completely New—Spiritually

In John 3:3, the Lord tells how the "Born Again" experience transforms our sin nature spiritually and secures our access to the Kingdom of God. This is our regeneration as we invite Jesus Christ into our lives by faith, and we receive a new internal nature that allows us to perform God's perfect will and show His favor.[8]

We are no longer spiritually dead, because the Helper, who now lives inside us, transforms us into "new" creatures (1 Corinthians 5:17). With our old life gone and defeated, our new life craves the Lord and His righteousness,

> Regeneration involves the illumination of the understanding, the consecration of the affections, and the rectification of the will. To use Paul's language, "Ye were once darkness, but now are ye light in the Lord" (Ephesians 5:8).[9]

We may not experience dramatic social or financial changes, but we possess a new spiritual nature that cancels our animosity toward God.

Flesh and blood cannot inherit the Kingdom of God (1 Corinthians 15:50). Our access is spiritual through transformed hearts. Once our hearts are changed, He then changes our standing as well.

God Declares Us Righteous

God gives us a new standing through justification. Here, by faith in Christ, God no longer sees vile sinners. He sees the righteousness of His Son, which makes us suitable for eternal fellowship with Him,

He was wounded for our transgressions, he was bruised for our iniquities: the chastisement of our peace was upon him; and with his stripes we are healed (Isaiah 53:5 AKJV).

We were guilty and condemned when we received His righteousness and glory. A sinless Jesus Christ died on our behalf to secure our new position and eternal fellowship. Now the Helper ensures we endure to the end.

🕊 *We Endure to the End*

We are kept by the power of God through faith unto our salvation ready to be revealed in the last time (1 Peter 1:5). We endure to the end because of His infinite power, providence, and preservation.

Our perseverance reflects the Lord's omnipotence and faithfulness in the lives of His precious children as Article Eleven entitled, "The Perseverance of the Saints," of the *New Hampshire Confession* describes,

> We believe the Scriptures teach that such as are truly regenerate, being born of the Spirit, will not utterly fall away and perish, but will endure to the end; that their persevering attachment to Christ is the grand mark which distinguishes them from superficial professors; that a special Providence watches over their welfare;

and that they are kept by the power of God through faith unto salvation.[10]

We endure because our focus is on Christ, whose providence watches over us. Providence is God's activity of providing for His people. As when Abraham did not have an animal sacrifice when Isaac asked what they were going to sacrifice to the Lord. Abraham responds, "The Lord will provide." The Lord provided, and as a result, Abraham names that location, "*Jehovah-jireh*" or "the Lord will provide" (Genesis 22:14).

Also, in Psalm 23:1, King David tells us how the Lord, as our Shepherd, provides all we need. In Matthew 6:8, Jesus tells us how our caring Father knows what we need, even before we ask Him. Thus, as our divine provider, God is more than able to supply all our needs according to His "riches in glory" (Philippians 4:19).

His preserving power keeps us as He implements His divine, comprehensive purposes and plans brought into being by His power and will,

> God acts in human history secretly and mysteriously for the good of His Elect people, using the free decisions and sinful activities of [humanity] for His own ends.[11]

We benefit from God's providence, which works all things together for our good (Romans 8:28). And we also benefit from His preservation that ensures His continuous administration and oversight, through which He maintains all the things He has created, along with their properties and powers with which He has endowed them.[12] It's God who preserves and sustains us forever,

> You alone are the LORD. You made the skies and the heavens and all the stars. You made the earth and the seas and everything in them. You preserve them all, and the angels of heaven worship you (Nehemiah 9:6 NLT).

We who confess Christ with our mouths and believe in Him with our hearts will endure to the end (Romans 10:9–10). Those who profess with their mouths but do not believe with their hearts will not endure because they are not of Christ,

> They went out from us, but they were not of us; for if they had been of us, they would have continued with us; but they went out that they might be made manifest, that none of them were of us (1 John 2:19 NKJV).

We who profess and believe find eternal hope, strength, and victory in Christ. As His chosen according to His foreknowledge, we progress toward a glorious destination together—Heaven.

🕊 *We Are Elect According to His Foreknowledge*

Jesus says we did not choose Him. He chose and appointed us. As His called and chosen according to His foreknowledge, we can find comfort knowing He calls and chooses—not us.

However, we can have even greater hope for the certainty of God's hand in the direction, purpose, and the ultimate course of our lives,

> God knew His people in advance, and He chose them to become like his Son, so that his Son would be the firstborn among many brothers and sisters. And having chosen them, he called them to come to him. And having called them, he gave them right standing with himself. And having given them right standing, he gave them His glory. What shall we say about such wonderful things as these? If God is for us, who can ever be against us (Romans 8:29–31 NLT).

One attribute of God, omniscience, is His ability to know perfectly and eternally "all things which can be known, past, present, and future. God knows how best to attain to His desired ends."[13]

Within the context of all the things God knows perfectly and eternally is His foreknowledge of our redemption in particular,

> The objects of [God's] foreknowledge are the free acts of men. Such knowledge is involved in the prediction of events,

> which either concern the free acts of men, or are dependent on them. If God be ignorant of how free agents will act, His knowledge must be limited, and it must be constantly increasing, which is altogether inconsistent with the true idea of His nature. His government of the world also, in that case, must be precarious, dependent, as it would then be on the unforeseen conduct of men. As the omnipotence of God is His ability to do whatever is possible, so His omniscience is His knowledge of everything knowable.[14]

God's ordering, calling, choosing, and predestining our human lives to become like His Son while at the same time preserving our ability to have total "free will" is something people continue to debate.

Rather than join this debate, suffice it to say our election is a mystery that reflects God's sovereign will and deliberate action. He is God, and it is His prerogative to choose what He feels is the best course for advancing His universe along with deciding the best means to fulfilling those ends.

Herein lies the mystery, He chooses us for salvation, but not in consideration of our moral and spiritual merit (since we have none). Jesus says God draws us to Him (John 6:44). Now He affirms we are His chosen. These ideas are not contradictory because God does not want us to perish. He wants us to come to Him (2 Peter 3:9).

Election is a wonderful display of God's sovereign will and wisdom He extends to *all people* who are willing to come to Jesus Christ (*my emphasis*),

> You were slain, and have redeemed us to God by Your blood out *of every tribe and tongue and people and nation* (Revelation 5:9 NKJV).

Unfortunately, "free will" also means there will be those who will reject God's gracious invitation as they ignore His Word, scoff at His teachings, spurn His Son, and resist the Helper's urgings.

Nevertheless, Calvary's cross still allows God's love and forgiveness to touch everyone equally. Christ will reconcile even the vilest of sinners to Himself without distinction. Nevertheless, it is incumbent upon us to accept His invitation freely and willingly,

> Behold, I stand at the door and knock. If anyone hears My voice and opens the door, I will come in to him and dine with him, and he with Me (Revelation 3:20 NKJV).

Those of us who hear His call and respond to it positively will comprise His Universal Church or the Bride of Christ.

🕊 We Comprise His Church

His chosen will comprise His visible Kingdom of God, His Bride, or the Church where the very powers of Hell cannot prevail (Matthew 16:18, Ephesians 5:32, Revelation 19:7–8 KJV).

The Greek word for church, *ekklesia* (Strong-G1577), combines two Greek words, *ek* (Strong-1537), denoting movement out of something into something, and *kaleo* (Strong-G2564), denoting an act of calling.[15]

We have been called out of the world to occupy His glorious invisible Kingdom, represented by His visible New Testament Church,

> But you are a chosen people, a royal priesthood, a holy nation, God's special possession, that you may declare the praises of him who called you out of darkness into his wonderful light. Once you were not a people, but now you are the people of God; once you had not received mercy, but now you have received mercy (1 Peter 2:9–10 NIV).

In this New Testament age, we are local microcosms of the Church Universal, the Bride of Christ, who gather regularly for, worshipping, reading and hearing God's Word (Bible), singing songs and hymns, prayer, fellowship, giving financially through tithes and offerings, and serving others without harm.

We also meet to observe the ordinances of Christ, baptism and the Lord's Supper, and we participate in every means of grace necessary for our spiritual life and prosperity.

In chapter two, we explored the Lord's Supper. But here, baptism is a visible testimony of the transforming, regenerating work the Helper performs inside us based on our faith in Christ.

In essence, baptism demonstrates our death to our old life and nature, symbolized by our burial or immersion under water and our rising out of the water to show we have a new Christ-centered life,

> Therefore, we were buried with Him through baptism into death, that just as Christ was raised from the dead by the glory of the Father, even so we also should walk in newness of life (Romans 6:4 NKJV).

We are the living examples of the undeniable truth that God can transform vile sinners into His holy people—from the inside out,

> Now there are many peoples in the world; the Christians, however, are a people with a special call and are therefore called not just *ecclesia*, "church," or "people," but *sancta catholica Christiana*, that is, "a Christian holy people" who believe in Christ. That is why they are called a

> Christian people and have the Holy Spirit, who sanctifies them daily, not only through the forgiveness of sin acquired for them by Christ, but also through the abolition, the purging, and the mortification of sins, on the basis of which they are called a holy people.[16]

The Helper confirms our Lord's "choosing and appointing" us by working within us to produce lasting fruit through greatly beneficial spiritual gifts He distributes for service within the church.

🕊 *We Have Beneficial Spiritual Gifts*[17]

The church is where we honor the Lord by serving each other using these eight core spiritual gifts.

❖**Helpers** share their time, talents, and resources to accomplish specific tasks to aid and assist others in need. They eagerly and faithfully demonstrate compassion and concern by responding to other's needs, often with a desire for anonymity, as extensions of Jesus' caring hands. We all need helpers to aid us in our time of need or distress (1 Corinthians 12:28).

❖Much like helpers, **Givers** also share their material resources to meet other's needs tangibly and meaningfully. Also, like helpers, they tend to prefer anonymity and do not expect repayment for their generosity. God has blessed them with the resources they compassionately and unselfishly give to help others in need. Thus, they understand fully that He will adequately repay them for their faithful work we all need in our times of distress. (Proverbs 3:27, Romans 12:8).

❖ The **Wise** have the ability to match problems with solutions, but from God's perspective. They function in ways that glorify God and astonish others. These men and women help our pastors and church leaders make critical spiritual, financial, and legal decisions that help to strengthen and sustain the church's operation (1 Corinthians 12:8, James 1:5).

❖ **Exhorters** use the Word of God to console, encourage, and remind us of God's love and purpose for our lives. The Helper gives exhorters the precise words we need to hear that testify of Christ and of His ongoing work in us and for us. They help us remember we are not alone because God is with us—forever. Through the Word of God, exhorters help us find renewed inspiration and motivation to continue serving the Lord and others faithfully (Romans 12:8).

❖ **Evangelists** share the good news of Jesus Christ in ways that make it easy for hearers to respond to the message positively. We all have a wonderful testimony of how the Lord redeems, provides, and is preparing our glorious future, and we share our testimonies with others. However, God calls specific people to serve as His evangelists locally and around the world to share the message of God's love and grace we all can experience through Jesus Christ, our Lord (Ephesians 4:11).

❖ **Pastors** nurture others toward spiritual maturity. Also called shepherds and bishops, they are the spiritually mature who serve under the leadership of Christ, the Good Shepherd, as both teacher and leader (Jeremiah 3:15, Acts 20:28, Ephesians 4:11, 1 Timothy 3:1–7, Titus 1:5–16).

As **Teacher**, pastors demonstrate the ability to explain Bible truths in ways that allow people to understand and apply them to everyday life. Teachers make the Bible "come to life" and so that it becomes relative and important to us. (Romans 12:7, Ephesians 4:11).

As **Leaders/Administrators**,[18] pastors provide effective and efficient oversight to the local church, using tact, vision, and prudence to maximize its resources, provide direction, and ensure its stability. Here, pastors free themselves from a secular worldviews by adopting a biblical worldviews to maintain the spiritual integrity, mission, and values of the local church. (Romans 12:8, 1 Corinthians 12:28).

Regarding "effective" and "ineffective" ministry, some are convinced that a flawed past enhances our Christian ministry and think people are more effective "relating" to others after living tragic lives of sin before coming to Christ. Although it is appropriate to share about our old life in contrast to our new life in Christ, ministry effectiveness is completely up to the Helper, who is at work in us.

While every Christian needs a support and accountability network to guard against moral and spiritual failure, people who've endured years of tragic abuse (either as the perpetrator or the victim) should seek clinical treatment in conjunction with their church-based, Christian discipleship program before they serve in leadership to lessen the risk of spiritual, physical, or emotional harm to others. Scriptural rules to follow here would be to take heed to yourself and do not appoint leaders hastily (1 Timothy 4:16, 5:22).

Others feel that church numerical growth, large edifices, solid capital, and notoriety are the "proofs" of effective ministry. However, important hidden indicators such as our hearts, our motives, and God's perfect will are disregarded or ignored. The Lord knows whether our hearts and motives are vile or pure, and He will perform His will accordingly. The Lord wants us to define our ministry's effectiveness from His perspective; herein lies what matters most.

Through Christian discipleship in a church setting, we can best identify and utilize our spiritual gifts. We also learn how to represent the Lord in a manner that reflects His love, humility, and noble character consistently as we operate under His unfaltering might.

The World's Opposition

Jesus gives His Disciples a somber warning of the extensive persecution that is forthcoming for those who follow Him,

> If the world hates you, keep in mind that it hated me first. If you belonged to the world, it would love you as its own. As it is, you do not belong to the world, but I have chosen you out of the world. That is why the world hates you. Remember what I told you: A servant is not greater than his master. If they persecuted me, they will persecute you also. If they obeyed my teaching, they will obey yours also (John 15:18–20 NIV).

Since the onset of sin in the Garden of Eden, there has been a striking distinction between God's people and the world. The first murder was perpetrated by unrighteous Cain, who killed his righteous brother Abel out of his petty animosity and jealousy (Genesis 4:1–8, Matthew 23:35, Hebrews 11:4).

From that day forward, there has been an adversarial relationship between the wicked and the righteous,

> The wicked have drawn the sword and have bent their bow, to cast down the poor and needy, to slay those who are of upright conduct…The wicked watches the

righteous and seeks to slay him (Psalm 37:14, 32 NKJV).

In our fallen and sin-cursed world, everyone is subject to these unseen spiritual forces,

> You used to live in sin, just like the rest of the world, obeying the Devil—the commander of the powers in the unseen world. He is the spirit at work in the hearts of those who refuse to obey God. All of us used to live that way, following the passionate desires and inclinations of our sinful nature (Ephesians 2:2–3 NLT).

Jesus knew of His betrayal, trial, and crucifixion at the hands of wicked men. But He also knew that wicked people would attack His Followers as well.

Thus, the Lord never intended us to establish a cozy affinity with the world or worldly things. (He wants us to enjoy all the good things this world has to offer—*but keep Him first.*) Instead, He warns us against it because we will invariably devote ourselves to them and lose our fervor for Him (Ecclesiastes 9:7–10, Matthew 6:24, 33, Luke 16:13).

Jesus warns against our cozy, compartmentalized living in His salt analogy in the Sermon on the Mount. There, He compares us to unsavory salt and asks the rhetorical question, "How can salt be made salty again?" Then He concludes that unsavory salt is not good for anything except to be thrown out and trampled underfoot (Matthew 5:13).

All that the world has to offer are the lusts of the flesh, the lust of the eyes, and the pride of life (1 John 2:16). Allegiance to the world causes us to lose sight of the cross, robs us of our love for God, and diminishes our desire to serve Him exclusively. Thus, friendship with the world is certain to make us enemies with God (James 4:4).

God wants no other gods before Him (Exodus 20:3). Although we are pilgrims on our way to our heavenly home, we often act like His fickle sheep, which can be easily distracted as well. We have one Master, Christ. Our attempts to serve two masters simultaneously will fail us disastrously.

Ultimately, our fallen, sin-cursed world is not looking for any more examples of double-minded duplicity and hypocrisy. It has all the poor examples of human failure it will ever need.

Instead, when the world looks at us Christians, it must see how fervently we love the Lord with all our hearts, souls, minds, and strength with a single-minded, single-hearted focus.

Jesus explains more about the Helper and how His presence will change our lives radically. We will explore these lessons in the next chapter.

Notes

[1] Augustus H. Strong, *Systematic Theology*, 31st ed., (Valley Forge: Judson Press, 1976) 796.

[2] Spiros Zodhiates, "καθαίρω," *The Complete Word Study Dictionary, New Testament*, rev. ed., (Chattanooga: AMG International, 1993) 792.

[3] J.P. Lange, "The Gospel According to John," *Commentary on the Holy Scriptures: Critical, Doctrinal and Homiletical*, Philip Schaff, trans., 7th ed., vol. 9, (Grand Rapids: Zondervan, 1980) 462.

[4] Consulting your medical care professional for fasting guidelines before fasting is highly recommended.

[5] Augustus H. Strong, *Systematic Theology*, 31st printing, (Valley Forge: Judson, 1976) 870.

[6] James Strong, "φίλος," "Dictionary of Greek Words," *Strong's Exhaustive Concordance of the Bible*, updated ed., 3rd printing, (Peabody: Hendrickson Publishers, 2009) 1681.

[7] For further discussion, see: Adam Clarke, "John," Clarke's Commentary: *The Holy Bible Containing the Old and New Testament*, new ed., vol. 5, (NY: Abingdon Press, 1966) 629, and Archibald Thomas Robertson, "The Fourth Gospel," *Word Pictures in the New Testament*, reprint, vol. 5, (Nashville: Broadman Press, 1960) 260–261, and Marcus Dods, 830–831.

[8] *"Born Again," "Second Birth," "In Christ," "New Birth,"* and *"Union with Christ"* are synonymous terms for the human and divine elements of our spiritual transformation. The human element (*conversion*) happens when we turn from sin (*repentance*) and turn to Christ (*faith*). The divine element (*regeneration*) is when the Helper enlivens (*quickens*) our spirits and makes us new creatures.

[9] J. M. Pendleton, *Christian Doctrines*, 33rd printing, (Valley Forge: Judson, 1976) 59.

[10] Edward T. Hiscox, "Perseverance of the Saints," *The Standard Manual for Baptist Churches* (Philadelphia: American Baptist Publication Society, 1951) 67.

[11] J.D. Douglas, Walter A. Elwell, and Peter Toon, "Providence," *The Concise Dictionary of the Christian Tradition: Doctrine, Liturgy, History*, (Grand Rapids: Zondervan, 1989) 309.

[12] Augustus H. Strong, *Systematic Theology*, 410-411.

[13] Merrill C. Tenney, "Omniscience," *The Zondervan Pictorial Bible Dictionary*, (Grand Rapids: Zondervan, 1967) 609.

[14] Charles Hodge, *Systematic Theology*, 3rd printing, vol. 1, (Peabody: Hendrickson, 2003) 400–401.

[15] James Strong, "ἐκκλησία," 1622.

[16] Martin Luther, *Martin Luther's Basic Theological Writings*, ed., Timothy F. Lull, (Minneapolis: Fortress Press, 1989) 540–541.

[17] This is not an exhaustive treatment, but a review of eight common and practical gifts that facilitate the local church's mission for "equipping the saints for the work of ministry, for the edifying of the body of Christ" (Ephesians 4:12 NKJV).

[18] The Helper gives people who are not pastors leadership and administration gifts for church service also.

Chapter Five

Chapter Five:
The Helper's Mission and Work

The Helper's Reproving Work

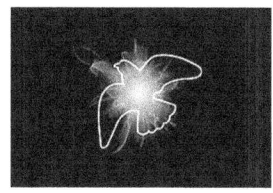
Jesus tells the Disciples that He is leaving and the Helper is coming, because they will need His reproving guidance and assistance to sustain the movement during the trying and turbulent times approaching them,

> I tell you the truth. It is to your advantage that I go away; for if I do not go away, the Helper will not come to you; but if I depart, I will send Him to you. And when He has come, He will convict the world of sin, and of righteousness, and of judgment: of sin, because they do not believe in Me; of righteousness, because I go to My Father and you see Me no more; of judgment, because the ruler of this world is judged. I still have many things to say to you, but you cannot bear them now. However, when He, the Spirit of truth, has come, He will guide you into all truth; for He will not speak on His own authority, but whatever He hears He will speak; and He will tell you things to come. He will glorify Me, for He will take of what is Mine and declare it to you. All things that the Father has are Mine.

Therefore I said that He will take of Mine and declare it to you (John 16:7–15 NKJV).

The Helper reproves by exposing the world of its sin, righteousness, and judgment. The Greek word used for reprove is *elegcho* (Strong-G1651), which is a bringing to light, reprove or correct, to shame, to expose, to set forth, to convict someone of something, or to point something out.[1]

The Helper reproves the world of its sin and discloses our means of righteousness through Christ while revealing how the Satan, the Prince of this world, has been defeated and condemned forever.

Reproving the World of Sin

The Helper enables the world to realize its sin. The Greek word sin, *hamartia* (Strong-G266), applies to all humans equally by showing how all our attempts to please God with good works, apart from Christ, will always "miss the mark."[2]

In other words, we are sin-convicted due to our aversion to Jesus Christ, which causes us to miss the ultimate end and scope of all life—God. Outside of Christ, life has no true purpose or meaning. With the absence of His divine truth in us, we manufacture our own truths (lie) for selfish, personal, or political gain.

We will not find fulfillment in social connections, social consciousness, recreation, wealth, industry, fame, or intellectual pursuits. Although some of these achievements are financially beneficial, they do not address the needs of our eternal souls satisfactorily,

> What good will it be for someone to gain the whole world, yet forfeit their soul? Or what can anyone give in exchange for their soul? (Matthew 16:26 NIV)

Invariably, these things do not satisfy our spiritual longing for God's acceptance and abiding love. Thus, the things we elevate to replace Him, including ourselves, become the gods we futilely worship and trust, leaving us spiritually bankrupt and unfulfilled,

> They have forsaken me, the spring of living water, and have dug their own cisterns, broken cisterns that cannot hold water (Jeremiah 2:13 NIV).

Sin causes us to live shallow lives hating God, disrespecting ourselves, and denouncing others through intimidation and hostile violence. Proud and privileged, we begrudge, vandalize, and plunder. Our aversion to God and godly things prevents our engaging in healthy relationships. As a result, we aimlessly chase relationships, never finding lasting fulfillment.

The government is not exempt either. In Jesus' day, Rome enforced emperor worship, which posed a serious threat to all Christians since it mandated they worship mortals as they worship Jesus, and violators were executed,

> The refusal of all Christians to participate in [Emperor Worship] precipitated violent persecution, for the Christians consistently objected to worshipping a human being. The polytheistic Romans, who could always add one more god to their list of deities, looked upon their refusal as a lack of proper recognition for the emperor and a distinctly unpatriotic attitude. Between these two viewpoints, there could be no reconciliation.[3]

In today's world, sin causes us to worship the "state" in the form of a godless Marxist-Leninist ideology people endorse around the world,

> At the core of its philosophy and conduct is the conviction and the oft-repeated announcement, "There is no God." The absence of God is not simply another acceptable philosophic point of view, among many others. Rather, it is the denial of the Christian claim—yes, the teachings of the Bible—that there is a just, holy, loving, and personal God who has created the universe and who presides over its continuance.[4]

Godless ideologies influence our politics, business, schools, colleges, media, and even the clergy, vainly promoting an empty utopian promise that we can provide for ourselves, apart from God. In other words, we have no need for Jesus Christ, God, or the Bible—*we are all we will ever need!*

It also enforces a censorship against biblically-centered ideals that contrast their "everything is relative" and "everyone is right" narratives. In this godless utopia, hostility and disrespect replace common courtesy and consideration, just as if the eschatological prophesy, "After that, [Satan] must be set free for a short time" (Revelation 20:3 NIV) is happening right before our eyes.

Workers on the Tower of Babel were likewise seduced by their own sin, pride, and arrogance,

> Come, let's make bricks and bake them thoroughly...Let us build ourselves a city, with a tower that reaches to the heavens, so that we may make a name for ourselves (Genesis 11:3-4 NIV)

As those builders failed, today's godless elitists fail because they refuse to acknowledge the universal, inherent sin-problem plaguing all of us,

> When you follow the desires of your sinful nature, the results are very clear: sexual immorality, impurity, lustful pleasures, idolatry, sorcery, hostility, quarreling, jealousy, outbursts of anger, selfish ambition, dissension, division, envy, drunkenness, wild parties, and

other sins like these (Galatians 5:19–21 NLT).

No person wants to live in a world where people think and act irresponsibly constantly. Yet, left to our own devices, we are doomed to experience it since we all commit sin. Ecclesiastes 1:2 teaches our human efforts are "futile and meaningless" because they do not offer us the forgiveness of sin and peace with God, which are essential to a spiritually fulfilling, eternal life.

To every sensitive heart, the Helper highlights our human frailty and sin, producing guilt and shame. Then, He points the way to righteousness through Christ.

🕊 Reproving the World of Righteousness

When His Father accepted Jesus' atoning sacrifice, He became our universal righteousness. The Greek word used is *dikaiosune* (Strong-G1343), to disclose all that which is "right" from God's vantage point—*not ours*. This is consistent with the quality of God's being, which is holiness.[5]

At the onset of His ministry, our Lord announced, "The Kingdom of God is at hand" (Mark 1:15). After selecting His Disciples, He presents the Beatitudes (Matthew 5:3–12) or the Kingdom of God lifestyle in His Sermon on the Mount, which His Followers will exhibit and disclose His righteousness to the world superbly.

🕊 *The Kingdom Characteristics—Beatitudes*

By our humility, or being **poor in spirit**, toward Jesus Christ, we possess the Kingdom. This is when our repentance (**mourning**) results in God's eternal consolation through His forgiveness of our sin.

With restrained human capacities under control or **meekness**, we inherit a world where God reigns forever and satisfies our yearnings as we **hunger and thirst for His righteousness**.

We are a people who show pity or **mercy** because we are the benefactors of His mercy. The Helper gives us **pure hearts**, which enable us to be **peacemakers** so that others can identify us as the children of God who abide in Him and will share in His majesty and splendor very soon.

The Lord Himself brings us His comfort when the world **reviles and persecutes** us or criticizes and mistreats us because we belong to Him. Even in the worst of circumstances, we can **rejoice and be exceedingly glad** because the rewards are great that await us in the Kingdom of Heaven.

In addition, we are the "salt of the earth," and "the light of the world" (Matthew 5:13–14) as the Helper radiates the Fruit of the Spirit from within us to season and preserve those around us as His moral, spiritual instruments of grace and love.

🕊 We Have Compelling Fruit of the Spirit

As we grow spiritually, we produce more Fruit of the Spirit (Galatians 5:22–23) with **love** as the centerpiece. Here, we are affable, courteous, and gracious as our **joy** yields a Spirit-suppled delight from our deeply fulfilling relationship with our Helper, in whom we have all we need for this life and the next.

We create and preserve **peace** with others as Jesus, the Prince of Peace works through us. We are **gentle** as we impart **goodness** into the lives of those we encounter around us.

Others witness our **faith** by our reliable dealings with people, as we express **meekness** or humble submission to the Lord's will in everything. With **temperance,** we show self-control when the old nature craves attention as we continue to persevere in all things through **long-suffering**.

Christ is our ultimate example of righteousness. Now, we have taken the charge to be His living examples as the Helper empowers right living in us and through us.

🕊 Reproving the World of Judgment

Judgment presents the idea of demarcation or separation. In essence, the world will be judged on what was to happen to the Lord within the next twenty-four hours on Calvary's cross. The Greek word *krisis* (Strong-G2920), is used for judgment.[6]

The concepts of judgment, separation, and Satan's doom are presented throughout Scripture,

> ❖Choose you this day whom ye will serve;...but as for me and my house, we will serve the LORD (Joshua 24:15 AKJV).

> ❖Then you shall again discern between the righteous and the wicked, between one who serves God and one who does not serve Him (Malachi 3:18 NKJV).

> ❖When the Son of Man comes in His glory, and all the angels with Him, then He will sit upon His glorious throne. All the nations will be gathered in His presence, and He will separate the people as a shepherd separates the sheep from the goats. He will place the sheep at His right hand and the goats at His left (Matthew 25:31–33 NLT).

> ❖I saw Satan fall from heaven like lightning!...I have given you authority over all the power of the enemy...But don't rejoice because evil spirits obey you; rejoice because your names are registered in heaven (Luke 10:18–20 NLT).

> ❖Then I saw an angel coming down from heaven with the key to the bottomless pit and a heavy chain in his hand. He seized the dragon—that old serpent, who is the

devil, Satan—and bound him in chains for a thousand years (Revelation 20:1–2 NLT).

The Helper continues to reprove the world of judgment ever since Christ emerged from the tomb and proclaimed He has all power both in Heaven and on the earth (Matthew 28:18).

He defeated the Enemy completely, and we are no longer subject to him—forever. *Amen!* Now, to fight our battles, the Helper supplies us with His powerful spiritual weapons to overcome the world.

Overcoming the World

Ours is an active vigilance in the Christian campaign. We are no longer spectators because Jesus has enlisted us into life-long service as this old and familiar hymn declares,

> Give of Your Best to the Master[7]
> Charlotte A. Barnard (1830–1869)

> Give of your best to the Master; Give of the strength of your youth; Throw your soul's fresh, glowing ardor, Into the battle for truth. Jesus has set the example; Dauntless was He, young and brave; Give Him your loyal devotion, Give Him the best that you have.
>
> *Refrain:*
> Give of your best to the Master; Give of

the strength of your youth; Clad in salvation's full armor, Join in the battle for truth.

Give of your best to the Master; Give Him first place in your heart; Give Him first place in your service, Consecrate every part. Give, and to you will be given; God His beloved Son gave; Gratefully seeking to serve Him, Give Him the best that you have.

(Refrain)

Give of your best to the Master; Naught else is worthy His love; He gave Himself for your ransom, Gave up His glory above. Laid down His life without murmur, You from sin's ruin to save; Give Him your heart's adoration, Give Him the best that you have.

(Refrain)

Jesus Christ is our Commander and Chief, yet He does not make us invincible. From the Disciples until now, Christians have endured fierce persecution and martyrdom,

Following their Savior in rapid succession fell many other martyred heroes: Stephen was stoned, Matthew was slain in Ethiopia, Mark was dragged through the streets until dead, Luke hanged, Peter and

Simeon were crucified, Andrew tied to a cross, James beheaded, Philip crucified and stoned, Bartholomew flayed alive, Thomas pierced with lances, James, the less, thrown from the temple and beaten to death, Jude shot to death with arrows, Matthias stoned to death and Paul beheaded.[8]

Hardship and persecution do not negate God's love for us, nor do they show His desertion because nothing can separate us from His love. In the final analysis, our persecution and toil remind us of sin's presence in our world, which contrasts His magnificent, sinless Kingdom we look forward to living in one day.

The momentary, "slight afflictions" we face now, prepare us for the massive, eternal "weight of glory" (2 Corinthians 4:17). Although confusing and uncomfortable at times, the progression of trials to reward has never disappointed,

> We can rejoice, too, when we run into problems and trials, for we know that they help us develop endurance. And endurance develops strength of character, and character strengthens our confident hope of salvation. And this hope will not lead to disappointment. For we know how dearly God loves us, because He has given us the Holy Spirit to fill our hearts with His love (Romans 5:3-5 NLT).

We will forget all our toil and suffering instantly, the moment we behold Jesus Christ in His full majestic splendor. Until then, we are steadfast and ever vigilant in pursuing our incorruptible inheritance by God's power. Our greatest challenges are not physical—they are spiritual. To combat these forces successfully, we must use *God's Armor.*

 *The Sustaining Spiritual Armor of God*

Ours is a life-long struggle, but not against flesh and blood,

> For we are not fighting against flesh-and-blood enemies, but against evil rulers and authorities of the unseen world, against mighty powers in this dark world, and against evil spirits in the heavenly places (Ephesians 6:12 NLT).

Jesus Christ gives His Followers the ability to be strong by standing firm in the power of His unfailing might as outlined in Ephesians 6:10–18.

To cover our torso, we securely fasten our belt or **Girdle of Truth** around our waist. It secures our body armor or **Breastplate of Righteousness** properly. We reveal His truth by our integrity and reliability as we perform noble acts that show He is working through us.

Our protective footgear or **Preparation of the Gospel of Peace** provides a firm and steady foundation for us to move quickly and sure. Our gospel of peace, "imparts the sense of freedom, relieves us of what burdens us, and gives us a spirit of courageous readiness for the battle with evil."[9] Here, the Helper gives us a steadfast faith in Christ along with the readiness of a prepared mind so that we can swiftly engage our Christian conflict with a gospel whose message is peace.

Our **Shield of Faith** quenches the fiery darts the Enemy (Devil) hurls at us as. In this way, our faith becomes the substance of things hoped for and the evidence of things not yet seen (Hebrews 11:1). Over time, our shield repels those things that distract or discourage our progress, allowing us to continue on our path to victory in Christ.

Our **Helmet of Salvation** protects our most important body part, our heads. Thus, we have no spiritual effectiveness unless we are Born Again. In other words, we cannot share a testimony we do not have or lead where we have not been. We become the "blind leading the blind" to our ultimate destruction and theirs (Matthew 15:14). (The Seven Sons of Sceva learned this lesson when the demonic spirit they were trying to repel left them battered, bruised, and naked in Acts 19:16.)

The Lord has given us one offensive weapon, the **Sword of the Spirit** (Bible). God says His words will accomplish His will and prosper where He sends it (Isaiah 55:11) Jesus successfully dispelled Satan when He was tempted by responding: "It is written" (Matthew 4:1–11). Victory is not in our human philosophies or opinions. It is in the precious and powerful Word of God.

Each day we study God's truths and promises contained in the Bible so that the Helper can call them to mind as we navigate life's uncertainties. Our diligent study and preparation allow us to share biblical truths with others that will greatly benefit them and us (Psalm 119:105, 2 Timothy 2:15).

Prayer is the weapon we use as we endeavor not to lose heart (Luke 18:1). The Helper aids us to pray without ceasing by interceding for us when we face those urgent moments when words fail to express our circumstances adequately (Romans 8:26, 1 Thessalonians 5:17).

Jesus commands us to pray to the Father directly in His name. We need no human intermediary since we now have direct access to the Father. Because of Jesus' name, God will acknowledge the prayers we offer for others and ourselves,

> In that day you will ask in My name, and I do not say to you that I shall pray the Father for you; for the Father Himself loves you, because you have loved Me, and have believed that I came forth from God. I came forth from the Father and have come into the world. Again, I leave the world and go to the Father...These things I have spoken to you, that in Me you may have peace. In the world you

will have tribulation; but be of good cheer, I have overcome the world (John 16:26–28, 33 NKJV)

We are more than conquerors when we exhibit Jesus' life and character,

> Yet in all these things we are more than conquerors through Him who loved us. For I am persuaded that neither death nor life, nor angels nor principalities nor powers, nor things present nor things to come, nor height nor depth, nor any other created thing, shall be able to separate us from the love of God which is in Christ Jesus our Lord (Romans 8:37–39 AKJV).

Ultimate victory is ours, and our eternal blessing is secure. He will keep us safe from Satan and his spiritual forces at work against us, just as He promises,

> I give them eternal life, and they will never perish. No one can snatch them away from me, for my Father has given them to me, and He is more powerful than anyone else. No one can snatch them from the Father's hand (John 10:28–29 NLT).

Jesus concludes His lessons of faith and offers His intercessory prayer for His Disciples and us today. We will explore His prayer in the next chapter.

Notes

[1] Walter Bauer, "ἐλέγχω," *A Greek-English Lexicon of the New Testament and Other Early Christian Literature* F. Wilbur Gingrich and Frederick W. Danker, ed., 2nd rev. ed. (Chicago: University of Chicago Press, 1979) 249.

[2] Spiros Zodhiates, "ἁμαρτία," *The Complete Word Study Dictionary, New Testament*, rev. ed., (Chattanooga: AMG International, 1993)130, and W.E. Vine, "Sin," *An Expository Dictionary of New Testament Words*, in *Vine's Expository Dictionary of Biblical Words*, rev. ed. (Nashville: Thomas Nelson, 1985) 576–577.

[3] For further discussion, see: John Foxe, *Foxe's Book of Martyrs*, 30th printing, Marie Gentert King, ed., (Old Tappan: Fleming H. Revell Company, 1977), and Merrill C. Tenney, *New Testament Survey*, 7th printing, (Grand Rapids: Wm. B. Eerdmans Publishing, 1980) 67.

[4] For further discussion, see: Dave Breese, *Seven Men Who Rule the World from the Grave*, (Chicago: Moody Press, 1990) 67, and William L. Reese, "Marxism," *Dictionary of Philosophy and Religion: Eastern and Western Thought*, 8th ed., (Atlantic Highlands, NJ: Humanities Press, 1980) 336–337, and William L. Reese, "Lenin, Vladimir Ilyich,"301.

[5] Spiros Zodhiates, "δικαιοσύνη,"458-462, and W.E. Vine, "Righteousness," 535.

[6] Spiros Zodhiates, "κρίσις," 889–891, and W.E. Vine, "Judgement," 337.

[7] Charlotte A. Barnard, "Give of Your Best to the Master," *Voice of Praise*, B.B. McKinney, ed., 12th Printing, (Nashville: Broadman Press, 1947) 286.

[8] For further discussion, see: J.M. Carroll, *The Trail of Blood*, Ross l. Range ed. (Lexington: Ashland Baptist Church, 1975) 11, and Philip Schaff, "The Great Tribulation," *History of the Christian Church*, reprint, vol. 1, (Grand Rapids: Eerdmans Printing Company, 1985) 376–390.

[9] S.D.F. Salmond, "The Epistle to the Ephesians," *The Expositor's Greek New Testament*, reprint, Robertson Nicholl, ed., vol. 3, (Grand Rapids: Wm. B. Eerdmans, 1980) 386–387.

Chapter Six

Chapter Six:
Jesus' Intercessory Prayer

Jesus Prays to be Glorified

Our Lord Jesus Christ, the great High Priest closes His public ministry with His three-part intercessory prayer. In the first section, He petitions the Father for His former glory, which He gives back to the Father,

After saying all these things, Jesus looked up to heaven and said, "Father, the hour has come. Glorify your Son so he can give glory back to you. For you have given Him authority over everyone. He gives eternal life to each one you have given him. And this is the way to have eternal life—to know you, the only true God, and Jesus Christ, the one you sent to earth. I brought glory to you here on earth by completing the work you gave me to do. Now, Father, bring me into the glory we shared before the world began (John 17:1–5 NLT).

The hour has come. The betrayer, Judas was on the way, and in just a few hours, Jesus would offer Himself to be mocked, humiliated, beaten, and crucified,

> I gave My back to those who struck Me, and My cheeks to those who plucked out the beard; I did not hide My face from shame and spitting (Isaiah 50:6 NKJV).

But, all humanity was in spiritual peril. Sin and death bound us, where there was no escape. Jesus' single magnificent act would change the course of our future once and for all.

Up to now, Jesus was like any other person spouting lofty ideals, performing magical tricks, and leading a group of misfits and non-conformists. Such behavior is common and ordinary…especially in today's world. (Although raising the widow's son, Jairus' daughter, and Lazarus from the dead were quite spectacular feats.) In addition, He was thirty-three years old, give or take—a relatively young man—with all His faculties; cut down in the prime of His life.

His claim to be God in human flesh, or the Son of God, along with His claim to be our only means of redemption were without validation to this point. Then, something happened that distinguishes Him from anyone who has ever lived—*He arose from the dead.*

 *Jesus Rose from the Dead*

Through His resurrection, God glorifies the Son and validates His authority over Satan, sin, and death, making Him the most significant person who has ever lived, and it ensures us that He will not disappoint those of us who put our faith in Him,

> By any and all standards, Jesus Christ has always been regarded as the greatest figure in human history. On any list of the world's greatest men, we always find at its head Jesus of Nazareth. Regardless of whether or not men acknowledge Him as Savior and Lord, they must pay tribute to Him as the world's outstanding man.[1]

Many refer to Jesus as a prophet or teacher. Some say He was a good man who died tragically. If death was all there was, we would be hopelessly lost.

But, *praise the Lord!* Jesus' death is not all that there was to know about Him. He also rose from the dead, and He left behind an empty tomb.

Although some have tried, we cannot ignore the implications of this historical fact.

❖ The empty tomb validates the Lord's claim to be the Son of God or God in human flesh and that He, the Helper, and the Father are one.

> I and my Father are one…I will pray the Father, and He will give you another Helper…the Spirit of truth…I will not leave you orphans; I will come to you (John 10:30, 14:16–18 NKJV)

❖ It confirms God has approved Jesus Christ's atoning sacrifice for our sin and solidifies the new and abundant life we have in Him forever.

> For God so loved the world that He gave His one and only Son, that whoever believes in Him shall not perish but have eternal life. For God did not send His Son into the world to condemn the world, but to save the world through him. Whoever believes in Him is not condemned, but whoever does not believe stands condemned already because they have not believed in the name of God's one and only Son (John 3:16–18 NIV).

❖ It shows the Father answered His prayer to be glorified most emphatically.

> Therefore God exalted Him to the highest place and gave Him the name that is above every name, that at the name of Jesus every knee should bow, in heaven and on earth and under the earth, and every tongue acknowledge that Jesus Christ is Lord, to the glory of God the Father (Philippians 2:9–11 NIV).

❖It proves and assures we will also experience a glorious resurrection, just as He has,

> And though after my skin worms destroy this body, yet in my flesh shall I see God (Job 19:26 AKJV).

❖It assures us we can pray, read/study His Word, abide by His commands, trust His promises, attend church, observe His ordinances, serve others, and strive toward spiritual growth knowing our actions are productive,

> Therefore, my dear brothers and sisters, stand firm. Let nothing move you. Always give yourselves fully to the work of the Lord, because you know that your labor in the Lord is not in vain (1 Corinthians 15:58 NIV).

The foundation of our Christian faith is the actual bodily resurrection of Jesus Christ. Because of it, we sorrow not as others who have no hope (1 Thessalonians 4:13),

> This is but natural, as Christianity must stand or fall with the resurrection. Christ "rose from the dead," has always been a cardinal article of faith in the Christian Church; for the defense of the faith and comfort to the Believers. The difficulties that beset denial are found in: (a) the

impossibility of explaining the empty grave; (b) the attitude of the enemies of Christ after the resurrection, revealing their helpless confusion; (c) the Disciples' sudden transition from hopelessness to triumphant faith; (d) the founding of Christianity in the world, which can be rationally accounted for only in view of the fact that Christ actually rose from the dead.[2]

Our Christian faith, history, and theology derive from the idea that Jesus Christ rose from the dead physically. Along with the Disciples we, His Followers today, universally accept this as fact.

Despite the two thousand years of skeptics, our Christian faith has never been a product of "lies, fraud, hallucinations, and sick minds." Courageous, clear-minded Saints of God continue to die for their faith in the Lord because they know Him to be authentic and eternal. Christian faith stands or falls with the resurrection of Jesus.[3]

Our Lord willingly died to pay for our sins, and He triumphantly rose for our justification. He ascended into Heaven, where He now sits at the right hand of God, interceding for us. Soon, He will return for us, and we will be with Him forever in His peace and love. *Hallelujah!*

Jesus Prays for His Disciples

In His second part, Jesus prays for His Disciples,

> I have revealed you to the ones you gave me from this world. They were always yours. You gave them to me, and they have kept your word. Now they know that everything I have is a gift from you, for I have passed on to them the message you gave me. They accepted it and know that I came from you, and they believe you sent me.
>
> My prayer is not for the world, but for those you have given me, because they belong to you. All who are mine belong to you, and you have given them to me, so they bring me glory. Now I am departing from the world; they are staying in this world, but I am coming to you. Holy Father, you have given me your name; now protect them by the power of your name so that they will be united just as we are. During my time here, I protected them by the power of the name you gave me. I guarded them so that not one was lost, except the one headed for destruction, as the Scriptures foretold.
>
> Now I am coming to you. I told them many things while I was with them in this world so they would be filled with my joy. I have given them your word. And the world hates them because they do not

belong to the world, just as I do not belong to the world. I'm not asking you to take them out of the world, but to keep them safe from the evil one. They do not belong to this world any more than I do. Make them holy by your truth; teach them your word, which is truth. Just as you sent me into the world, I am sending them into the world. And I give myself as a holy sacrifice for them so they can be made holy by your truth (John 17:6–19 NLT).

Jesus spent three and one-half years teaching His Disciples what they needed to know to continue His work. The Lord saw Simon and changed his name to Peter (Greek, *petros,* or "rock." Strong-G4074). The name Peter would forever remind him of the "rock-solid leader" the Lord saw, who would lead the Believers after His departure.

This characteristic was evident when Jesus warned Peter that Satan desired to sift his faith like wheat. After the denials, Peter repented and the Lord restored him and assigned him to feed His precious sheep (Luke 22:31–32, John 21:15–17).

Peter helped the New Testament church to flourish during its infancy by articulating its mission and message. Ultimately, the Disciples' efforts to lead a faith movement turned the world upside down (Acts 17:6).

Jesus asks the Father to make them holy (sanctify) through His truth. The Greek word used for sanctify is *hagiazo* (Strong-G37), a verb that denotes the process of making holy; to purify, separate, consecrate mentally and ceremonially.[4]

Jesus also states God's Word is truth. The word used here is *logos* (Strong-G3056), which can refer to a spoken or written word, or it can refer to Jesus Christ, the pre-existent, personified Word of God (John 1:1).[5]

Noted Old Testament theophanic appearances of the Logos, some as the Angel of the Lord, show how He intervenes in human lives as God,[6]

- Adam, Eve, and Cain (Genesis 1–4)
- Enoch and Noah (Genesis 5–6)
- Abraham and Isaac (Genesis 12:7, 17:1, 18:1; 26:2)
- Jacob (Genesis 28:12–15)
- Moses (Exodus 33:11)
- Balaam (Numbers 22:31)
- Joshua (Joshua 5:13–15)
- Gideon (Judges 6:11–27)
- Manoah and his wife (Judges 13:3–27)
- David (2 Samuel 24:16–17)
- Solomon (1Kings 3:5; 9:2, 2 Chronicles 1:7; 7:12)
- Isaiah (Isaiah 6:1)
- Shadrach, Meshach, Abednego, and Nebuchadnezzar (Daniel 3:25)
- Zechariah (Zechariah 1)

Thus, all His discussions with His Disciples, on this His last evening especially, bore exceptional weight to be trusted, because they were words from the very mouth of God,

> No created being could speak as Christ here speaks. He begins exhorting His Disciples to have the same faith in Him which they had in God. He went to prepare Heaven for them and would return and take them to Himself. The knowledge of Him is the knowledge of God. He who had seen Him had seen the Father also for He and the Father are one. He promised to send them the [Helper] to abide with them permanently; and that He would manifest Himself to them as God manifests Himself to the Saints, revealing to them His glory and love, and making them sensible of His presence. He would continue to be to His Church the source of life; union with Him is as necessary as the union of a branch to the vine. The [Helper] sent by Him would reveal the things of Christ, rendering the Apostles infallible as teachers, and giving divine illumination to all Believers.[7]

As the Word, Jesus Christ was the reflection of the Father in human form. Before His incarnation, He was God, eternal, self-existent, creator of all things, life, light, truth, wisdom, and glory.[8] Then the eternal Word of God became flesh,

> The Word became flesh and made his dwelling among us. We have seen his glory, the glory of the one and only Son, who came from the Father, full of grace and truth (John 1:14 NIV).

Jesus Christ is the means by which God's divine truth is revealed to humanity. In other words, He is the entire substance of God's Word—from Genesis to Revelation. Thus, the Lord prays that the Father will separate and use the Disciples for the distinct and holy purpose of being His emissaries to communicate His good news around the world

Under the Helper's inspiration and illumination, the Disciples would communicate the glorious message of Jesus Christ so that the world would know the Lord alone is the Most High over all the earth, and there is only one name on earth given unto us whereby we must be saved (Psalm 83:18).

We call Him Jesus because He saves us from our sin. God did not send His Son into the world to condemn it, but to save it. So that if anyone is in Christ, they become new creatures; the old has passed away; behold all things are new (Matthew 1:21, John 3:17).

Jesus Prays for His Followers

Jesus closes His prayer by interceding for all those who will follow Him because of His Disciples' testimony and the Helper's revealing work,

> I am praying not only for these disciples but also for all who will ever believe in me through their message. I pray that they will all be one, just as you and I are one— as you are in me, Father, and I am in you. And may they be in us so that the world will believe you sent me.
>
> I have given them the glory you gave me, so they may be one as we are one. I am in them and you are in me. May they experience such perfect unity that the world will know that you sent me and that you love them as much as you love me. Father, I want these whom you have given me to be with me where I am. Then they can see all the glory you gave me because you loved me even before the world began!
>
> "O righteous Father, the world doesn't know you, but I do; and these disciples know you sent me. I have revealed you to them, and I will continue to do so. Then your love for me will be in them, and I will be in them (John 17:20–26 NLT).

Jesus prayed for those of us today who believe the Disciples' message. It is because of their faith and courage we can experience our resurrected Savior today,

> That He would grant you, according to the riches of His glory, to be strengthened with might through His Spirit in the inner man, that Christ may dwell in your hearts through faith; that you, being rooted and grounded in love, may be able to comprehend with all the Saints what is the width and length and depth and height to know the love of Christ which passes knowledge; that you may be filled with all the fullness of God. (Ephesians 3:16–19 NKJV).

Jesus prays that as His Believers, we will be one with each other, with Jesus, and the Father. Ours is a unified faith and message that reveals God answered His prayer. We belong to each other, and we belong to Christ—and He belongs to the Father.

In chapter two, we explored our unity under a new love mandate. Here we extend our unity and love to become family—a Christian family—with perfect, eternal unity that will forever reveal the matchless wisdom and power of God,

> We have been adopted into an eternal family of God. As children of God and

> joint heirs with Christ, we have the privilege of sharing both in His sufferings and in His subsequent glory. God gives us the privilege of walking the same path Christ walked, enduring sufferings in this life that we may also receive great glory in the life to come. Because we are God's children, our relationship with each other is far deeper and more intimate than the relationship that angels, for example, have to one another. For we are all members of one family. [9]

The Helper enables us to share in common many fulfilling moments that strengthen our resolve to follow Christ. Daily, we experience how God loves, protects, and provides us with everything we need. We grow ever confident that He directs our steps, and will never leave or forsake us,

> Be strong and of good courage; do not be afraid, nor be dismayed, for the LORD your God is with you wherever you go (Joshua 1:9 NKJV).

The Helper also solidifies our faith in God and His Word so that we grow to rely on His eternal promises and providence instead of our subjective thoughts and fickle emotions. He will provide us with all the spiritual resources we need to live for Christ victoriously.

The Bible presents people who have fruitful and fulfilling relationships with the Lord that begin early and last throughout their lives. This is truly the Christian heritage and legacy to strive for, a special and unique witness that shows everyone we are one—even as Jesus is one with the Father. Those of us who follow this pattern by coming to Christ early, learning God's Word, attending church, learning from spiritually mature teachers and pastors in discipleship, and using our gifts in service are living testimonies of His miraculously transforming power.

The Helper enables us to grow in grace and the knowledge of our Lord and Savior Jesus Christ to share God's Word properly so that He can attract, convict, convince, and inspire others unto right thinking and living (2 Peter 3:18). Then, we can present His righteousness, grace, and love through our worship, service, and fellowship. The Helper also works in us to share the life and message of Jesus Christ effectively. Here, we sanctify the Lord God in our hearts. Then we can offer a timely response to those who ask us about the unfailing hope within us, with meekness and godly reverence (1 Peter 3:15).

Ultimately, it is because of this one incredible evening, that with the aid of our Helper, we can do all things through Christ, who strengthens us both now and forever (Philippians 4:13).

What a Wonderful Savior!

Notes

[1] H.I. Hester, *The Heart of the New Testament*, 35th ed., (Nashville: Broadman Press, 1981) 5.

[2] Rev. E. McChesney, "Resurrection of Christ," *Unger's Bible Dictionary*, 18th printing, Merrill F. Unger, ed., (Chicago: Moody Press, 1972) 920–921

[3] Bill R. Austin, *Austin's Topical History of Christianity*, (Wheaton: Tyndale House, 1983) 42.

[4] James Strong, "ἁγιάζω," "Dictionary of Greek Words," *Strong's Exhaustive Concordance of the Bible*, updated ed., 3rd printing, (Peabody: Hendrickson Publishers, 2009) 1599.

[5] Walter Bauer, "λόγος," *A Greek-English Lexicon of the New Testament and Other Early Christian Literature* F. Wilbur Gingrich and Frederick W. Danker, ed., 2nd rev. ed. (Chicago: University of Chicago Press, 1979) 477–479.

[6] For further discussion, see: Arthur B. Fowler, "Theophany," *"The Zondervan Pictorial Bible Dictionary*, (Grand Rapids: Zondervan, 1967) 846, and J.D. Douglas, Walter A. Elwell, and Peter Toon, "Angel of the Lord," *The Concise Dictionary of the Christian Tradition: Doctrine, Liturgy, History*, (Grand Rapids: Zondervan, 1989) 25.

[7] Charles Hodge, *Systematic Theology*, 3rd printing, vol. 1, (Peabody: Hendrickson, 2003) 507–508.

[8] Charles Hodge, vol. 1, 504-506, and J.P. Lange, "The Gospel According to John," *Commentary on the Holy Scriptures: Critical, Doctrinal and Homiletical*, Philip Schaff, trans., 7th ed., vol. 9, (Grand Rapids: Zondervan, 1980) 49–57.

[9] Wayne A Grudem, *Systematic Theology: An Introduction to Biblical Doctrine*, (Leicester, England; Grand Rapids, Michigan: Inter-Varsity Press; Zondervan Pub. House, 2004) 741.

About the Author

Floyd Bland has given his life to serving the Lord Jesus Christ as a pastor, teacher, ministry leader, and administrator. He serves within his local church and for Not Of The World Ministries, Inc.

Floyd helps strengthen others in their faith in the Lord and in their relations with others by offering sound, practical, Bible-based interactive models for Christian living.

Floyd's other publications include *The Christian Heritage: God's Answers for a Searching World*, *Radical Forgiveness Through the Eyes of Jesus*, *Five Things Every Christian Must Know*, and *Oh For The Joy! Forgiven and Free in Christ*.

Floyd is married to his best friend and helpmate, and together they have two grown children and a grandson.

www.ingramcontent.com/pod-product-compliance
Lightning Source LLC
Chambersburg PA
CBHW071004080526
44587CB00015B/2335